KOREAN PREACHING

KOREAN PREACHING

An Interpretation

JUNG YOUNG LEE

Abingdon Press
Nashville

KOREAN PREACHING: AN INTERPRETATION

Copyright © 1997 by Abingdon Press

All rights reserved.

This book is printed on acid-free, recycled paper.

Library of Congress Cataloging-in-Publication Data

Lee, Jung Young.
    Korean preaching: an interpretation / Jung Young
    Lee.
        p.   cm.
    Includes bibliographical references.
    ISBN 0-687-00442-X (alk. paper)
    1. Preaching—Korea.   I. Title.
BV4208.K6L44   1997
251'.0089'957073—dc20   96-42571
                                                                                CIP

Scripture quotations, unless otherwise indicated, are from the New Revised Standard Version Bible, copyright © 1989, by the Division of Christian Education of the National Council of the Churches of Christ in the United States of America.

97 98 99 00 01 02 03 04 05 06—10 9 8 7 6 5 4 3 2 1

MANUFACTURED IN THE UNITED STATES OF AMERICA

I faithfully dedicate this book to

Yesu

who said, "The time is fulfilled,
and the kingdom of God has come near;
repent, and believe in the good news."
(Mark 1:15)

CONTENTS

PREFACE

When I was invited to present a workshop at "Proclamation 91" in Nashville, Tennessee, a few years ago, I was asked by Abingdon Press if I would be interested in writing a book about Korean American preaching. I was delighted because I had been thinking about writing about this topic for some time. After accepting the challenge, I intentionally visited as many Korean American churches as possible to observe various preaching styles, and the problems that Korean preachers were experiencing in America. Since I teach in a theological seminary that more than eighty Korean students attend, I have been deeply concerned with the problems of Korean preaching in America. These Korean students have been candid about their views of the Korean church in America, their frustrations in working with senior pastors, and the many other difficulties that they encounter as youth ministers, associate ministers, or ministers of small congregations. I have also received input from the doctoral students, many of whom have been in ministry for many years. But perhaps the honest sharing of my concerns about preaching with my most intimate Korean ministerial friends has been the most helpful in preparing me to write this book.

I do not intend for this book to provide a simple survey of Korean American preaching. My personal observations of Korean preaching and my conversations with Korean preachers have assisted me in reaffirming the perception of

Korean preaching that I have developed over the years from preaching in Korean congregations in various areas of the country. So this book is a presentation of my own ideas about Korean preaching based on my experience, and the information that I have received from various Korean preachers who have been grappling with the future of Korean ministry. I do not pretend to know everything about Korean preaching, nor do I speak for anyone else. I present my candid views of Korean preaching and my vision of the future possibilities for Korean ministry in this country. My intent here is to offer a critical study of Korean preaching, which may arouse controversy among some Korean ministers, and suspicion among white American ministers who have been impressed by the expansion of Korean American ministry in this country. This book is intended not to be a "how-to-preach" resource, but instead a "what-to-do" and "what-is-to-be-done" resource. This is perhaps the best way to express my critical evaluations as well as my personal vision of Korean preaching in America. My hope is that this book might serve as a catalyst for readers to reassess the present practice of their preaching ministry and to find new ways of improving it.

What qualifies me to write such a book? My qualifications come out of my experiences of preaching in Korean American congregations as well as in white American churches. Although my experience of teaching continuing education for Korean American ministers for several years at a denominational seminary has taught me a great deal about Korean preaching in America, the main assumptions in this book are based upon my own experiences of preaching to Korean American congregations. In 1969 I started a Korean congregation in Columbus, Ohio, which was the first Korean congregation in the Midwest, except for the First Korean United Methodist Church in Chicago. After serving that congregation for several years, I started another Korean congregation in Grand Forks, North Dakota, where one of the largest bases for the United States Air Force is located. The majority of this congregation consisted of the Korean wives of U.S. service-men, although a few Korean church families were related to the university in town. Later, I expanded my preaching ministry to the Fargo community, which was about seventy miles away. A few of the sermons I preached to these con-gregations were included in the book *Sermons to the Twelve* (Abingdon Press, 1988). In addition to my preaching experi-ence in Korean American congregations, I have also served white American congregations in Toledo, Cleveland, and Dayton, Ohio. My preaching experience in both Korean and white American congregations has given me the ability to view Korean preaching more objectively and critically than those preachers who have served only Korean congrega-tions. Teaching in a theological seminary for the last several years has continued to fuel my interest in Korean preaching. Although there are many reasons for this continued interest, the one that motivated me the most to write this book was the sense of urgency for a critical assessment of this topic, the need for a blueprint of the future for Korean preaching.

In organizing the book, in chapter 1 I begin with an attempt to explain the importance of understanding Korean preaching in America. Chapter 2 presents Korean preaching in the context of Korean culture. Since religious tradition is the essence or soul of a culture, I explain the traditional Korean religions, including shamanism, Buddhism, and Confucianism. Each of these traditions is discussed in light of the pietistic and evangelical faith of the early Christian missionary movement. The chapter then lays the ground-work for the cultural context of Korean preaching. Chapter 3 depicts the concept of Korean preaching as the embodi-ment of the worship service. The thing that differentiates preaching from lectures or storytelling is that preaching is always done in the context of worship. Worship and preach-ing are inseparable. Special attention is also given to prayer, music, and scripture in worship. Chapter 4 describes distinc-tive emphases in Korean preaching. Here I relate Korean preaching to the traditional background of the Korean people. Chapter 5 explains the position of Korean preachers in their congregations and in Korean American society. The authority of preachers in the patriarchal and hierarchical structure of Confucian society and in the spiritualization of shamanic tradition is discussed. Chapter 6 presents Korean preaching in transition from a first-generation congregation to a second-generation congregation. The dangers and possibilities of a transitional phase are also discussed. Chapter 7 summarizes the distinctive characteristics of Korean preaching and its possible contributions to the American church at large.

In preparing this book, I am most grateful to the members of the various Korean congregations that I have served over the years. They became my teachers and my preachers as well. I am also grateful to the many Korean ministers who shared their concerns for and aspirations for preaching with me. I give special thanks to those Korean preachers who were students in my continuing education classes, my close friends who are serving various Korean congregations, and those seminary students who willingly shared their frustrations and hopes for their future preaching ministry. Most of all, I am deeply indebted to the Professional Books editorial staff at Abingdon Press, who not only encouraged me to undertake this project, but also supported me through its completion. Without their assistance this book would not have been written. I am also thankful to Ann Shaw and Judith Kurth, my research assistants, who proofread the material. Finally, I am grateful to my family. Whenever they came back from a Korean worship service, they encouraged me to write more about Korean preaching. In many cases they found Korean preaching distasteful to their spiritual palates. It is time to add spices, salt, and hot pepper to Korean preaching.

Madison, New Jersey
January 1996

CHAPTER 1

WHY KOREAN PREACHING?

The Curiosity of Korean Preaching

One of my primary reasons for writing this book is that most American preachers and seminary students are unknowledgeable about Korean American preaching despite the rapid growth in Korean congregations in America. During a clergy continuing-education workshop I presented on "emerging themes in contemporary Korean preaching" at a theological seminary a few years ago, the American ministers in attendance admitted that Korean preaching was something mysterious to them and to many other American preachers. Although the Korean American church is growing faster than any other church population in this country, American clergy understand neither the Korean congregation nor Korean preaching. "There must be something that we don't know about Korean preaching," said one of the ministers in the workshop. Many American preachers are curious to find out what Korean preaching is, because the Korean church *is* known as one of the fastest-growing churches in this country.

In comparison with other Asian immigrants in this country, Koreans are extremely religious and almost fanatical in their devotion to the life of the church. This fact is borne out by the unprecedented growth of the Korean American church. The demographic picture of Korean congregations shows evidence of this impressive growth by the more than

2,600 Korean American congregations that have been established in the last twenty years.[1] According to the *National and International Religion Report*, these congregations include: 300 United Methodist churches, 250 Presbyterian churches (USA), 230 Korean Presbyterian churches in America, and 650 Southern Baptist churches.[2] Although the number of congregations is striking, more than 50 percent of these churches are categorized as small churches, which consist mainly of a few extended families. They are, therefore, known as family churches and have a membership of less than sixty.[3] The medium-size church has between 60 and 200 members, and includes about 20 or 30 percent of all Korean congregations. Large churches have memberships of between 200 and 800 people and make up about 10 percent of all Korean churches. There are about twenty-five or thirty megachurches, with a thousand or more members. The thing that impresses most American church leaders is that the smallest Korean congregation has the potential to grow so rapidly that it can become a megachurch within several years. A church in my neighborhood illustrates this point. The church is only a few years old, but has grown so quickly that it now has more than a thousand members, and its own worship center and large education wing. It is the largest "new" church of its denomination in our area, with an annual budget of more than a million dollars.

Seeing the rapidly expanding Korean congregations in America and knowing that more than 70 percent of all Koreans in America are in one way or another affiliated with a Korean congregation, many non-Korean preachers are curious to know what Korean preaching is like.

In spite of this curiosity, there are few books or comprehensive articles dealing with the topic. I believe that this is one of the first attempts to uncover the reality of Korean preaching and the types of problems that the Korean preacher must overcome in his or her preaching ministry. The observations presented here are my candid personal judgments on Korean preaching and the Korean church in America. Some points that I offer may offend some Korean ministers in this country. Although my critical judgments and challenges to Korean preaching may displease some, I am confident that many serious and honest Korean preachers will agree with my assessment. I have attempted to present the positive as well as the negative aspects of Korean preaching, so as to help readers form their own opinions.

The Importance of Korean Preaching in a Multicultural Society

Knowledge of Korean preaching is important because we live in a multicultural and multiethnic society. For many years preaching courses did not presuppose multicultural congregations. When I attended seminary in the late 1950s, the standard for preaching was based solely on the European tradition. During that time distinctive preaching styles or emphasizing black preaching or Hispanic American preaching were not taught. The preaching styles of ethnic minorities were never even mentioned in the seminary classroom. Whether we were Asian American, Hispanic American, or African American, we were not taught or even encouraged to develop a unique mode of preaching that would fit into the context of our own congregations. Drastic changes have occurred in preaching philosophies due to the wide recognition of our pluralistic and multicultural society. We are obliged to recognize the importance of distinctive preaching styles existing in different ethnic congregations. Because preaching is a form of giving recognizable shape to the divine presence,[4] preaching must take cultural and ethnic contexts seriously.

Korean preaching is one of many topics that must be taken seriously in the multicultural mosaic. This mosaic is clearly evidenced by the changing demography of ethnic minorities in this country. The ethnic minority population is presently growing faster than the population as a whole, and there is speculation that "by the end of the next century there will be a new majority population in America—a majority of minorities."[5] For example, in the Bronx there has been a 32.2 percent decrease in the white population, but a 5.6 percent increase in the black population, a 32.4 percent increase among Hispanics, an 87.8 percent increase among Asians, and a 45.4 percent increase in various other ethnic groups. In Bergen County, New Jersey, which is regarded as one of the most prestigious living areas in the state, there has been a 10.6 percent decrease in the white population compared with an increase of 18 percent in the black population, 73 percent in the Hispanic population, 165.6 percent in the Asian population, and 23 percent in all other ethnic groups.[6] These broad shifts in demography among ethnic minorities have facilitated the inevitability of a multicultural society. And in this new mosaic society, the cultural distinction of ethnicity affects both the Christian life and the preaching ministry of the church.

In many ways Asian culture has already blended into the landscape of American culture. Many of us enjoy kimchi in Korean restaurants, sushi in Japanese restaurants, and wonton soup in Chinese restaurants. We drive Hyundais which were made in Korea, and Hondas or Toyotas which were manufactured in Japan. We listen to stereos and use computers which were made in Asia, and watch Asian movies on television. The evening news is broadcast in different languages for a diverse audience of ethnic viewers. Students are taught martial arts from Korean instructors, kung fu exercises from Chinese masters, and flower arranging from Japanese teachers. Many aspects of Asian culture have been integrated into American life. And although the news media keeps us informed about what is happening in Asian American communities, many of us are unaware of what is happening inside the Asian church. The Korean church, the fastest-growing segment of the Asian church, must be understood, in particular, just as we have learned about the elements of Asian culture.

Korean Preaching and Improving Working Relationships

Understanding Korean preaching can improve the working relationship between Korean American churches and white American churches. Most American ministers who attend my workshops are in some way involved in Korean ministry. Either they share their facilities with Korean congregations, or their churches are located near a Korean congregation. One of the most difficult issues that surface in a working relationship between a Korean congregation and an American congregation is the sharing of a facility. In most cases, it is the American congregation that shares its church structure with the Korean congregation, since most Korean congregations start out with only a small group of members that need a place to conduct worship services and other meetings. The problem occurs when the Korean congregation begins to grow rapidly, and begins demanding more building space to meet its preaching and social life needs. Moreover, the Korean congregation is very active, and does not meet just once or twice a week but almost every day. For example, there may be early morning prayer services each morning, Wednesday evening services, Friday night Bible study groups, along with a Sunday afternoon service following the eleven o'clock worship service of the American congregation. The Sunday afternoon service generally lasts more than an hour, sometimes even two hours, and then there is a fellowship time which lasts another hour or two. Many American ministers do not understand why the Korean people use the church building so frequently, and for so many hours each week. Since most Korean pastors do not speak English well, they may not communicate with American preachers as often as they should and misunderstandings develop. In addition, many American people do not like the smell of kimchi (pickled cabbages), which are served with almost every Korean meal. Cultural misunderstandings combined with a lack of knowledge about the Korean congregations can create enormous problems in two churches' working relationship. Sometimes these problems can easily be resolved if the American congregation becomes informed about Korean preaching and the Korean congregation. When renting church buildings to a Korean congregation, American congregations should anticipate active and full use of the church buildings.

Another serious problem in the working relationship between Korean and American preachers exists at the conference or synod level. For example in The United Methodist Church most bishops, district superintendents, and other ministers who hold leadership positions simply do not understand the distinctive characteristics of Korean preaching and ministry. So these leaders rely on a Korean advisor or advisors to provide them with the information that they need to make decisions in regard to Korean ministry. In some cases, the advisor exercises enormous power in influencing these decisions. However, one of the greatest difficulties that these leaders face is placing Korean preachers in churches. Many of the qualifications that are applied to the appointment of American pastors in United Methodist churches are not appropriate for Korean preachers or Korean congregations. Korean preachers and their congregations are so closely connected that the removal of a Korean preacher often results in the dispersal of his or her congregation. Many times the Korean congregation completely dissolves when its preacher is removed. Moreover, the standard that white Americans use for securing a preacher for a church and the standard that the lay leaders of the Korean congregation employ for receiving a preacher are so different that exhaustive consultations and negotiations are needed for a final agreement on a new preacher for a Korean congregation. There are numerous problems that Korean-speaking congregations present to denominational churches. For example, for the most part denominational hymnbooks and worship resources are never used in the Korean church. In planning programs for church regional conferences, the needs of Korean congregations are never considered because the planners lack an understanding of the distinctive aspects of the Korean church. Many Korean preachers do not stay within these church organizational structures, because they do not see the relevance of these activities and programs to their ministry. If they are required by church law to stay within these boundaries, then the Korean pastors usually gather in a small, separate group. In a way, the Korean church is like a small ghetto within the larger church. Some of these problems could be resolved if American ministers in leadership positions were aware of the differences in Korean preaching and ministry. This book may be helpful in informing them of the characteristics of Korean congregations and the problems that Korean preachers face in working with American preachers at various levels of the church in this country.

The Contribution of Korean Preaching

Understanding Korean preaching is also useful for American preachers in reassessing their own preaching ministry. Many mainline Protestant churches confront numerous problems which need to be overcome. The continual decline of their church rolls and the ineffectual presence of their ministry in the lives of many Christians warrant an examination of their preaching ministry. Although each congregation, especially each ethnic congregation, has its own distinctive context that must be considered in preaching, several aspects of Korean preaching offer opportunities to the revitalization of preaching ministries in mainline churches.

Understanding their own preaching better can help Korean preachers in America. I do not write this book simply to shed light on what Korean preaching is all about. As I said in the preface, in the depth of my heart, I want to assist Korean preachers in critically reassessing their preaching ministry and to provide a new vision for their future ministry in this country. I also want to give young and idealistic Korean preachers challenges that inspire the creative and imaginative use of cultural roots in their preaching ministry. The contribution of their preaching ministry in fact enhances preaching ministry at large.

Korean Preaching and Theological Education

Finally, a knowledge of Korean preaching is important to assist theological schools in training Korean preachers in this country and providing a comparative study in preaching and pastoral ministry. We live in a pluralistic society, where a multicultural approach to theological education is crucial. In our theological seminary we emphasize a multicultural approach to almost all academic and practical disciplines. Preaching should be no exception. The constituency of our student body also mandates a multicultural approach to our theological education. Almost half the students in one of my required courses last year belonged to an ethnic minority; about 25 percent were Korean students, and about 15 percent were black and Hispanic students. More ethnic minority students are enrolled in the seminary to prepare for ministry. That is why the resources we use to teach them also need to reflect a multicultural perspective. Korean preaching adds to those resources that represent the multicultural dimensions of theological education.

In the multicultural approach to preaching, first of all, it is crucial for Korean theological students to learn a type of preaching that is appropriate in Korean congregations. They must be aware of the pitfalls and advantages of Korean preaching practiced in this country. A critical examination of Korean preaching in light of other preaching is needed in order to improve Korean preaching in the future. We must allow theological students an occasion to use their creative imaginations to enrich their preaching ministry. Understanding Korean preaching helps students as well as preachers in the field to recognize the distinctive cultural contribution that ethnic preaching is making. Certainly, Korean preaching will add a new dimension to a multicultural approach to preaching and provide a comparative study in homiletics in theological education.

CHAPTER 2

UNDERSTANDING THE KOREAN CONGREGATION THROUGH HISTORY AND CULTURE

Since the essence of preaching is to communicate the gospel, an understanding of the relationship between the communicator and those receiving the message, or between the preacher and the congregation, is critical. Preaching presupposes knowing one's congregation. Even a television evangelist wants to know what kind of congregation watches the telecast. Knowledge of the educational, occupational, and economic background of the congregation, as well as their foundational faith orientations, is an important aspect of preaching. However, even more important than an awareness of listeners' educational or economic situations, is an understanding of their historical, religious, and cultural background. Understanding the ethnic background of a Korean congregation is particularly important for Korean preaching, because Koreans in America form a distinctive ethnic group. Ethnicity is often a more basic and fundamental element for understanding the thinking and behavior of a Korean congregation than are the individual educational or economic backgrounds of its members.

A small congregation that I served for many years illustrates the importance of the cultural and religious orientation of ethnic people. The congregation consisted of two categories of Korean Americans: those who belonged to the local university community, such as professors and students and their families; and the Korean wives of American servicemen from the nearby Air Base, whose average education did not exceed the fourth grade of public school in Korea. Each of these groups had its own distinctive lifestyles and thought patterns, and like water and oil, they did not seem to mix. The groups had nothing in common other than being Koreans. In order to communicate the gospel to these two entirely different groups, I preached using simple words and phrases that everyone could understand. And even the scripture was read in such a way that the members with minimum education could understand. The people from the university wanted sermons with intellectual challenge, but the less-educated women from the Air Base wanted (and needed) something else. My preaching had to satisfy the needs of both groups. This was not an easy task. I was able to address this challenge by stressing symbolism in my preaching. I used symbols which are common to the various Korean cultural and religious backgrounds with which every Korean congregant could identify.[1] These Korean religious and cultural symbols not only created a bridge between the two groups, but also helped both groups to better understand the gospel.

A knowledge of the distinctive historical and cultural background of Korean ethnicity is also important for communicating the whole gospel to a Korean congregation. Teaching mathematics or natural sciences does not require an understanding of the differing backgrounds of one's students, but preaching the gospel involves more than the intellectual and cognitive aspects of life. It also involves the emotional life of the listeners. Preaching speaks to the total commitment of people.

The Korean congregation I began in Columbus, Ohio, about twenty-five years ago, was only the second Korean church in the Midwest. Because I was a full-time teacher of religion at a Methodist college and was the only ordained Korean in that area, I often asked guest speakers to fill the pulpit. One Sunday I invited an American missionary to speak who had spent more than twenty years in Korea. He spoke Korean very well, and everyone in the congregation was amazed at his proficiency with the language. After the service, however, a few people told me that despite his excellent Korean, the missionary's sermon had not touched their hearts. "It was a good sermon," they said, "but there was something lacking." I knew that what was lacking was the cultural element. Because he did not have a history and culture in common with that of the Korean people, he could not fully share the Korean ethos, in spite of his excellent message.

As a Korean in America, I too feel inadequate when preaching to an American congregation. I cannot fully communicate the gospel to them, because of my cultural and ethnic difference. My preaching cannot touch the subtle emotional life of the American people. Although I have lived in America for many years, I still do not fully understand the American sense of humor, the jokes, or the strange slang expressions of Americans. When people laugh, I often feel out of place. The lack of understanding also occurs as a result of certain mannerisms.

To become an effective preacher it is important to learn to think, to feel, and to act as a part of the congregation. Thus, understanding the cultural and religious background of an ethnic congregation is essential for effective preaching.

The Christian Background of the Korean People in America

Although Christianity was introduced in Korea by Korean laymen more than two centuries ago, the actual impact of the Christian faith was not felt until the American Protestant missionaries arrived, a little more than a century ago.[2] In spite of its relatively brief period of development in Korea, Christianity has already become a leading Korean religion. More than 25 percent of the total population of South Korea are Christian.[3] The rapid growth of Christianity in Korea, combined with the unsurpassed development of technological and industrial resources, has helped to make South Korea one of the most highly Westernized countries in Asia. Today, Christianity seems to overshadow traditional Korean religions such as shamanism, Buddhism, and Confucianism, all of which had flourished in Korea for centuries before the arrival of Christianity. That same wildfire spirit of Christianity is exhibited in the lives of Korean immigrants in North America.

The Korean people in America are different from most other Asian people in America because of their Christian background. Their immigration history began with Christianity. The first Korean immigrants (except for a handful of students who came to the United States as political refugees) were members of a congregation in Inchun, headed by the Reverend George H. Jones, a Methodist missionary, and came to Hawaii as sugar plantation workers.[4] Other American missionaries also encouraged Koreans to emigrate to Hawaii. And as soon as they arrived in Hawaii, they set up congregations to worship together. It is often said: "When two Japanese meet, they set up a business firm; when two Chinese meet, they open a Chinese restaurant; and when two Koreans meet, they establish a church."[5] Everywhere there are Koreans in America, you will find a Korean church.

25

About 70 percent of the Koreans in North America are churchgoers.[6]

In 1965, new U.S. immigration laws were passed which opened America's doors to many Koreans. The chaos and unsteady political situation in Korea after the Korean War caused many Koreans, especially those who were well educated and connected overseas, to emigrate to North America.[7] Although most Korean men were the heads of their families, had received a Western education in Korea, and had held highly reputable positions there, they discovered that they were almost completely dysfunctional in America because of the enormous difficulties they faced stemming from linguistic, racial, ethnic, and cultural conflicts. In the midst of their suffering, dislocation, and identity crisis, Koreans sought and found an oasis in the church, a place where they could meet with other Koreans, speak their own language, and comfort themselves in the strange milieu of America. The church was for them the community of deliverance: It was "the heart of Korean American life."[8] Thus, the Korean American church began to revive after many years of internal conflict over the policy toward relations with the Korean national independence movement and with maintaining the status quo after the Korean liberation.[9]

During this period Korean ministers became more than just preachers, counselors, or prophets. They were also social workers, entertainers, and chauffeurs, helping their congregants find jobs and places to live, and so on.[10] Korean ministers became all things to all people. However, as Korean immigrants began to acclimate to their new country, establish businesses, and develop ways of coping with American life, the church's burden lessened.

Now as the Korean church approaches the twenty-first century there is a need to focus on the church's future, especially the future congregations of second- and third-generation Koreans, and to reach out to the American mainstream. In this transitional stage, Koreans in America seek to establish their identity as a distinctive ethnic group, whose existential meaning is to make a unique contribution to the lives of North American people. In order to accomplish this, however, the Korean church must change its emphasis from a fundamentalistic approach to a contextual approach, and from a one-sided spirituality to a holistic understanding of the gospel.

The theological orientation of the Korean church is based on the teachings of early missionaries, which are even today regarded as orthodox by most Korean churches. These teachings stress puritan ethics, such as no drinking, smoking, or dancing. Since the Korean church believes that a genuine Christian must have a "born again" experience, there is heavy emphasis on saving the souls of those who have become lost in the evil of the world. This kind of theological orientation has in the past provided the Korean people with a sense of security and protection from the constant threat of historical, political, and social instability that occurred after the introduction of Protestant Christianity. Korea had struggled for more than thirty years to liberate itself from colonization by Japan. When Korea was relinquished by Japan in 1945, it became divided into North and South Korea. Five years later, the Korean War took countless human lives, destroyed properties, and shattered the trust that Koreans had as one people. Korean spiritual and cultural traditions were bankrupted by Japanese rule, Communist ideology in the north, and capitalistic materialism in the south. During this time there was no time of peace and security for Korean Christians to develop their own perspective on theology or to liberate themselves from the exclusive and fundamentalistic theology that the early missionaries had brought to them. Although the indigenization of theology, such as minjung theology, is a recent phenomenon among theologians, the majority of Korean churches can still be characterized as conservative and evangelical, people whose faith is based on biblical inerrancy.

The same conservative and fundamentalist faith was imported to America when Koreans immigrated. In other words, the Korean people brought back to North America the exclusive, evangelical faith that the early American missionaries took to Korea more than a century ago.[11] Several years ago an American friend had an opportunity to visit a Korean revival meeting. He later told me, "Although I do not know Korean and did not understand what they were saying, I felt that I was actually participating in a revival meeting during nineteenth century America. I have read about it; now I have witnessed it."[12] Because Koreans in America are insecure and isolated from mainstream society due to barriers related to their communication skills and cultural and racial understandings of Western society, the exclusive and fundamentalistic approach to religion continues to appeal to them. In order to protect themselves from the seemingly hostile and alienating environment of their new country, immigrants voluntarily isolate themselves as a religious group by joining the Korean church in America. For these immigrants the church becomes their temporary haven, offering them a sense of identity as part of a community, and providing a family atmosphere that fosters their social life and serves as a status-building community among Korean immigrants in America.[13] Although the Korean church has served its members as a transitional instrument to adapting to American life, many ministers have attempted to use the tradition of their exclusivist faith to isolate their congregations permanently from American society at large. The more that immigrants are bound by this kind of theological orientation, the more they are isolated from the main society. The Korean church, therefore, must move beyond offering a faith of exclusive isolationism, to become an agent for transforming not only the church itself but also the Korean people in America.

The Korean church in America must become the "Korean American" church. In the same vein, first-generation Koreans must transform themselves into Korean Americans, just as trans-generational and second-generation Koreans see themselves as Korean Americans.[14] To be a Korean American means to have simultaneously Korean religious and cultural traditions and American religious and cultural traditions.[15] The exclusive Christian faith of the Korean tradition, which rejects other faiths such as shamanism, Buddhism, and Confucianism (which are all part of Korean history and culture), also then rejects Koreanness.

The task of Korean preaching, therefore, is to bring together the living faith of Christianity, which is the faith accountable to praxis, and the historical heritage of those other religions, which have been foundational for Korean culture. Understanding the Korean congregation is, then, more than understanding the theological orientation of the Korean church. It also means understanding other religions in Korea. Let us, therefore, turn our attention to the traditional religions of the Korean people.

Korean Shamanistic Tradition

Shamanism *(mutang)* is regarded as the foundation of Korean culture, because it is an indigenous religion which deeply penetrates the ethos and life of the Korean people. Other religions, such as Buddhism, Confucianism, and Christianity, were introduced to Korea from outside and became part of the Korean tradition, and shamanism was often victimized by these religions. Shamanism, having a primitive form of religious expression, may seem to have vanished in the technological and industrial society of Korea today, but it still lives in the hearts of the Korean people and is expressed in their lifestyle.[16] A former classmate who visited Korea about twenty years ago was amazed by the Korean people. He said, "Koreans are genuine human beings. They laugh when they are happy, and they cry when they are sad. I wish I could be like them." I told him that

Koreans can truly laugh and truly cry because they are children of Dangun, a great shaman, who is regarded as the ancestor of the Korean people.[17]

Although shamanism was the basic building block of Korean civilization, it was rejected and persecuted by other, newer religions, especially by Christianity. Shamanism is not only primitive in appearance, but its adherents also believe in many spirits and gods, particularly ancestral gods. Because of this belief in spirits, shamanism was called idolatry by Christians. The animistic and polytheistic tendency of shamanism was certainly not entertainable by the monotheistic Christian religion. Thus to be a Christian meant rejecting shamanism. When I was a child, I was told the story of my great grandmother's conversion to Christianity. She brought out of her house all the ritual instruments and images of shamanism she possessed and burned them in public to demonstrate her commitment to the Christian faith.[18] By rejecting shamanism, however, Korean Christians are rejecting their own culture, and they lose an important part of their identity as Koreans.

Like many Koreans in North America, I wanted to find my identity as a Korean American. I returned to Korea to rediscover my cultural heritage, to re-experience firsthand what it means to be Korean. I attended many shamanic rituals, not simply as an observer but as a participant. I learned to sing, to dance, to drink rice wine, to eat food from the shamanic altar, to laugh and to cry with other Koreans as a Korean. I consulted shamans for my fortune and followed their instructions. I came to respect their divine images as cultural expressions, although without any religious commitment to them. I learned to liberate myself from the rigid rules and categories of conventional life. In learning spontaneity, I felt that I was truly free. To exist meant to be free. Freedom and spontaneity were true expressions of the shamanic ethos that Koreans inherited. In shamanism, I discovered how I was different from Americans, and I began to discover a new identity that has helped me find meaning in my life in America.

In recent years minjung theologians have studied shamanism and tried to integrate it into Christianity.[19] However, shamanism is already a part of the Korean Christian experience. Most of the so-called successful ministers who have huge Korean congregations preach sermons which are basically shamanistic in character. The emphasis in Korean Christianity on healing, on charismatic appeals in preaching and prayers, on material blessings through spiritual power, and on the experience of ecstatic trance during worship are all results of shamanistic influence. However, shamanistic influence did not change the external form of Korean Christianity. Shamanism as an internal character of the Korean ethos will never disappear, but will continue to reappear in different forms in contemporary life, for it is the native religion of the Korean people. As Dong-sik Ryu, one of Korea's most prominent theologians, remarked, the Korean mind-set is basically shamanistic.[20] Understanding shamanism, therefore, is essential for preaching to a Korean congregation.

Korean Buddhist Tradition

It is impossible to talk about Korean history and culture without mentioning Buddhism. Buddhism came to Korea the fourth century A.D.,[21] and was the official state religion until Confucianism was adopted during the Yi dynasty in the fourteenth century. Along with shamanism, Buddhism became part of the tradition which nurtured the Korean way of life. Under Buddhism, a brilliant civilization arose in Korea during the Three Kingdoms period, the Unified Silla era, and the Koryo dynasties. Korean emissaries were sent to Japan to propagate Buddhism. Even today the ancient form of Korean Buddhism is observed in the Nara area, where the

Buddhist movement began in Japan. Korea prospered under Buddhism for more than a thousand years. Many beautiful paintings, sculptures, buildings, ceramics, and literary works which bear the characteristics of Korean Buddhism can still be found throughout Korean society. If shamanism was the basic building block of Korean civilization, then Buddhism refined that civilization.

In seeking to find my identity as a Korean in America, I also wanted to know the Buddhist aspect of my heritage. Instead of exploring Buddhism through books, articles, or films, I decided upon a more personal participation, Buddhist monastic life. I visited many temples to become acquainted with ancient Buddhist civilization. I spent a few weeks at Haein Temple studying Buddhism with other Korean scholars and laymen. Each day was begun by rising early, at about four o'clock in the morning, and attending an early morning service. By the sound of the temple bell, the main hall was filled with monks and laymen. The candlelight and incense, the recitations of sutras, the uniform responses of the congregation, and the meditation which constituted the morning service are still vivid in my mind. Returning from the service, we prepared food and ate together as a community of believers, or Shangha. Life was wholly a ritual: thought, movement, and even existence, were the rites of life. Mindfulness was the key to action, and compassion was the ultimate merit that motivated us for the service of others. Every day hours were spent meditating in the lotus posture, and listening to lectures given by senior monks. We learned to be in touch with the earth and how to deal with silence. By detaching themselves from the worldly life, Buddhist believers may eventually enter into Nirvana, the blessed state of existence. We were moved by the ideal of the Bodhisattvas who, having attained all the qualities needed to enter the blessed state, refused nevertheless to enter because of their compassion for the world. The Bodhisattvas then return to this world in various forms of existence to help others attain enlightenment. Whenever we met the Buddhist monks, they called us "Bodhisattvas," just as Paul called Christian believers "saints."

We listened to sermons expounding the Dharma (the law) by a famous Zen master, and were allowed time to approach him with questions. We were deeply moved by the profundity of the Buddhist philosophy of life, which is practiced in every moment of life. Ordinary life in turn became sacred through mindfulness, which is the fruit of meditation, and eventually every act became a meditation. Whenever I took the time to reflect on my own inner self, I realized how Buddhistic I had always been. Until immersing myself in Buddhism, I did not know why I loved to spend hours alone in contemplation and silence. I began to realize that these traits were a result of my Buddhistic heritage. In other words, Buddhism was no longer a strange religion for me once I realized that I was actually a product of it.

I began to wonder why Korean Christians rejected Buddhism. Christians referred to Buddhism as a godless religion, or atheism, because early Buddhists did not believe in God. Later, many different sects arose and divine images were introduced into Buddhism. In fact, the most popular sect of Buddhism, known as the Pureland Buddhism, made Buddha a deity. Many of the divine images and statues of Buddha in the temple displeased me, but I had to accept that they were ways of understanding Buddhist teachings. These images and statues had no religious significance for me, but what I found meaningful was that Buddhist teaching had given the Korean people a new perspective of life. Eventually, I came to appreciate Buddhism and was proud of being a part of the Buddhist tradition in Korea. I also discovered that my Christian faith was enriched by the Buddhist way of life. Buddhist teaching added a new dimension to my Christian faith.

Like shamanism, the Buddhism that Christianity rejected became a part of the Korean way of life, and Christianity, as a historical religion, has been forced to recognize that part of

Korean history which is also a part of the Buddhist heritage. And because Korean Christianity is a part of Korean history and civilization, it cannot be free from Buddhist influence. Thus, Korean Christians may reject Buddhism consciously but they practice it unconsciously. In this respect, they are Buddhist Christians. The service of early morning prayer in the Korean church was influenced by the Buddhist tradition. Korean Christians emphasize prayers wherever they go and whatever they do. As soon as they come into a house, a church, or any other place, the first thing they do is pray. Everything begins and ends with prayer. Although the evangelical and pietistic influence on the Korean church may have much to do with the habit of praying, the intensity and the manner of the prayers are distinctively Korean. It is often said that meditation and prayers are the way of the Christian life. In addition to prayer, most Korean Christians emphasize the experience of suffering, which is, according to Buddhist teaching, the inevitable consequence of human existence. The idea of Mirukbul, the future Buddha, which is very popular in Korea, supports Korean Christians' understanding of the second coming of Christ. Many other aspects of Buddhist philosophy are found in the life of Korean Christians. One of the ingredients that makes the Korean congregation distinctively different from the American congregation is the Buddhist tradition. Although many sermons are evangelical and exclusive in tone, they still contain a Buddhist ethos and philosophy of life.

Korean Confucian Tradition

Confucianism ruled Korea for five hundred years. When Yi Sung-gae established the Yi dynasty (which lasted until the Japanese annexation of Korea in the early twentieth century), he declared Confucianism the national religion. But Confucianism was actually more than a religion; it became the norm of the sociopolitical system. Therefore, it is often said that Koreans are more Confucianistic than is Confucianism. Koreans took Confucianism, especially orthodox Neo-Confucianism, so seriously that it became not only a philosophy or a religion but also the dominant political, social, and moral instrument.[22]

The heart of Confucianism that sustained the Korean people was its focus on ancestor worship. Christian missionaries and their followers were ruthlessly persecuted and murdered because of their refusal to practice ancestor worship.[23] While the Catholic church has since softened its position on ancestor worship, the Protestant church has continuously resisted it. Because Confucianism is deeply entrenched in the life of Korea, ancestor worship is still one of the most sacred rites in the mind of the Korean people; it is the soul of the Confucian culture and tradition with which most Korean people identify themselves. Although Korean Protestants refused to accept ancestor worship, they did not renounce it but Christianized it. *Ch'u-sok,* the national day of ancestor worship, occurs in the fall. It is similar to the Christian Thanksgiving Day. Fresh fruits and food from new crops are dedicated to ancestral spirits and shared by families and relatives. However, it is more than a day of thanksgiving; it is a time when Koreans visit family burial sites to commune with dead ancestors.

One of my most pleasant memories from my early childhood in Korea is of a *Ch'u-sok.* It was a beautiful autumn day. Our family took food and wine and placed them before our ancestral tomb. We bowed down before the tomb, like children bowing before their parents on New Year's Day. Then my father read a few verses from the Confucian liturgy. After the ceremony and while we were sharing the food we had brought, my father told stories about our grandfather. It meant a great deal to me to learn about my ancestor and to experience his presence with us on that day, and it resulted in a true experience of communion.[24]

Although Confucianism has been closely connected with ancestor worship, it is essentially a way of life governed by five relationships: between father and son, husband and wife, elder brother and younger brother, old and young, and the ruler and the ruled. These relationships are vertical or hierarchical in order. Among them, the relationship between father and son is the key to all other relationships in life. The essence of the father-son relationship is filial piety, which becomes the cornerstone for familial, social, and political life. It is said that when the father is no longer father and the son is no longer son, the nation will not survive.[25] The so-called rectification of names is important in defining the positions and stations of human existence, for unless we know exactly where we belong in life, confusion of roles arises, and a failure to maintain the functional efficacy of vertical relationships in society exists. This is why when one Korean meets another, he or she always asks personal questions such as: How old are you? What is your occupation? How much money do you earn? How many children do you have? What are they doing? These questions are often offensive to Americanized Koreans or second-generation Koreans. However, for most Koreans, knowing their place or position in relation to others is essential for socialization. By knowing their relationship with others, each can act and speak properly. For example, the Korean language has honorific expressions for those who rank high. Preachers in the church occupy the most respected position and are expected to exercise the authority vested by the nature of their occupation. However, this can also tempt them to become authoritarian, or even dictatorial figures in their congregations.

Confucian virtues have strong ethical dimensions, which include honor, honesty, sincerity, generosity, compassion, respect, and obedience. Education is meant to nurture these virtues and is thus a means of succeeding in life. For example, the old Chinese civil service examination based on the Confucian classics, which include many stories that illustrate the importance of learning, has been re-introduced in Korea. A socially insignificant or politically unknown person could one day become a prime minister if he passed the civil service examination with the highest distinction. Inspired by such possibilities, many people have spent their lives studying the Confucian classics.

Education remains important to the Korean people. Americans often do not understand why Koreans are almost fanatical about education. Most Koreans want to attend the best schools and to attain the highest academic degrees. Whenever they meet new people, they almost always ask: "What school did you go to? What schools do your children go to? What degrees have you received?" The Korean attitude toward education has been shaped by the teaching of Confucius, who was a great teacher. In Korean congregations it is typical for many subgroups to form around where members of the group went to school. These "alumni" groups can be a great asset to congregational life, but they can also hinder its growth, because they can become exclusive and reject fellowship with others.

It is beyond the scope of this chapter to describe every aspect of the Confucian tradition that deeply penetrates the life of the Korean people. By observing the social and ethical behaviors of the Korean people, it is possible to get an idea of Confucianism as practiced in Korea. However, the Korean people are more than Confucians. They are also Buddhists, shamans, or Christians. Many religious traditions are brought together in the life and thoughts of Koreans. Thus, Koreans are basically syncretic.

Let me illustrate this syncretic tendency. A few years ago, I learned that my brother who lived in Korea was dying. I immediately flew to Seoul to try to see him before his death. When I got there, he was already in a coma and died shortly after my arrival. Following his death, a Christian group came to his home and sang hymns, offered prayers, read scriptures, and preached a brief sermon. As soon as the Christian group left, a Buddhist monk came and offered incense, rang bells, and recited sutras for a few hours. An altar was set up according to the shamanistic custom. My brother's portrait and a tablet inscribed with his name were placed on the top, according to the Confucian tradition. Tables were filled with food, and arranged in specific directions, and then Confucian liturgies were recited. The children, relatives, friends, and other visitors honored his spirit by bowing down before his portrait on the altar. The burial site was chosen by shamans who specialized in geomancy; mourners wore Confucian gowns. For the funeral march, the casket was decorated with flowers forming the Buddhist symbol,[26] and my brother's portrait was carried by his oldest son.

My brother's death rite is a beautiful way of illustrating the coexistence of the many religious practices in Korea. My brother's first son was a Christian, his wife was a Buddhist, his father was a Confucian, and all of them shared the shamanic custom. In this service of the dead, all of these religious practices complemented one another to make the event meaningful to all participants. I, a Christian, also became a Buddhist, Confucian, and shamanist simultaneously in this event of honoring my dead brother. Through this experience, I became deeply conscious of the syncretic aspect of the Korean mentality. While syncretism has been given a negative connotation in Christianity, it is, for Koreans, a strength. It allows us to hold our faith without excluding other faiths. Syncretism means harmonizing religious traditions, rather than attempting to blend them. The Korean identity, thus, is not found in any one religious tradition. To be a Korean means to be inclusive of many religious traditions. It is important to recognize the presence of other religious traditions in the worship, music, prayers, preaching, and other activities of the Korean Christian life. As preachers we must be sensitive to these religious heritages, which can make Korean preaching enriching rather than debasing, and challenging rather than compromising.

The New Identity Crisis for Koreans in America

Koreans in America now confront new and different issues in their search for their identity. Finding identity in Korean roots alone is not enough. In America, Koreans are a minority group living in a dominant culture that does not fully accept them as equals, because of their racial and cultural differences. This problem of identity is serious for second-generation Koreans, who have already accepted the dominant culture as the norm of their lives. They are Americans because they were born in America, but they are not always accepted as Americans. Korean Americans are neither Koreans nor Americans, but are both Korean and American at the same time. They are in between two worlds. Even though first-generation Koreans identify themselves strongly with their root culture, they must also deal with the dominant American culture of which they are a part. Isolating themselves in Korean neighborhoods, in large cities such as Los Angeles or New York, does not solve the problem of their identity as Korean Americans. No matter how well they might be acculturated into American society, they are still Koreans or foreigners in the eyes of most white Americans. The identity crisis created by cultural and racial differences must be overcome, and is one of the most urgent tasks that a preacher must address with a Korean congregation.

The Korean congregation is both a homogeneous and a heterogeneous group. It is homogeneous because its members are of the same racial and ethnic background, but it is also a heterogeneous group because it includes many different subgroups formed around regional differences,[27] religious orientations, educational or occupational levels, generational gaps,[28] or extended families.[29] The positive interaction of subgroups may provide a dynamic and creative force for transforming the lives of both individuals and groups in the congregation; however, they can also serve as a divisive force within the congregation.

The Korean congregation is a custodian as well as a microcosm of Korean cultural and religious traditions in America. Because shamanic, Buddhist, and Confucian traditions have been a part of Korean culture, it is impossible for the Korean Christian to ignore these traditions. The syncretic Korean mind that harmonizes different religious and philosophical traditions can be regarded as a great asset in a multicultural and multiethnic society. This harmony of diverse traditions must be achieved in the name of Christ, who broke down the partition between Jews and Gentiles, between male and female, and between East and West. Preaching must be a message of liberation and hope for marginalized Koreans in America. Unity in Christ and diversity in culture seem to be the central message of God's kingdom on earth.

The creative use of the inner dynamic which is deeply rooted in the pluralistic religious orientation of the Korean people can make Korean preaching a truly exciting and challenging experience in American life today.

CHAPTER 3

KOREAN PREACHING IN THE CONTEXT OF WORSHIP SERVICES

Preaching and Worship Services

Although preaching has a certain style and content that differentiates it from, for example, a lecture, the one thing that makes preaching truly distinct from other forms of oral delivery is that its context is always worship. Preaching is not preaching unless it is done within the context of a worship service.[1] In fact, preaching is more than merely a part of the worship service; it is, in fact, a worship service. Every act of worship can be regarded as preaching. Prayers, music, hymn singing, reading scriptures, the citation of creeds, and the attitude of a congregation are all forms of preaching. Each action conveys the Word of God in its own form and style. Since the sermon is not "a free-standing piece,"[2] it must be carefully arranged and selected to express the central message that the preacher is attempting to convey.

Let me illustrate the interrelatedness of the worship service and preaching. In the summer of 1992, I was a member of a group which gathered at the foot of one of the famous "Diamond" mountains of North Korea early one morning.[3] When I looked up at the tall and majestic mountain, I was deeply inspired and sensed the wonder of divine presence. The peak was so high that we could not see anything except the cloud that covered it. Climbing that mountain was like ascending to heaven by Jacob's ladder, a route which stretched infinitely upward. The path that led us upward paralleled a stream of clear and crystal water, which flowed down from the peak. All we heard, other than our own voices, was the sound of water in the flowing stream. When we came to a waterfall, we heard a thunderlike sound. Where the stream was deep, we heard nothing but silence. We carefully followed the rugged path which had been charted by thousands of people before us over many thousands of years. There were many inspiring and beautiful vistas on our way. We stopped at these sites for rest and to enjoy the scenic beauty of our journey. Occasionally we scooped the cool and crystal water to our mouths to quench our thirst. It took almost all morning to climb to the top, where the water sprang up from the ground and flowed downward toward both east and west. When we reached the zenith, we saw the amazing vitality and grandeur of the water, surging from the top of the mountain. We stayed there for more than twenty minutes, observing the inexhaustible power and the impeccable mystery of the mighty spring. We were thrown into an awe-inspired ecstasy. Feeling transformed by that experience, we began to descend the mountain along the same path we had ascended.

If we compare the experience of climbing that mountain to the experience of a worship service, the water symbolizes the Word of God flowing down through the stream. Preaching in the Protestant tradition represents the peak experience of the worship service. It is like the experience of seeing the mystery of the water surging up at the top of the mountain. Preaching then helps the congregation confront the Word of God which is always available, like the water that flowed through the stream. And like climbing the mountain along the stream of water, we also hear and sense the presence of God in every moment of our worship experience. It is manifested in music, like the sound of shallow water, in meditation, like the silence of deep water, and in taking bread and wine, like the drinking of water to quench our thirst. The path we followed is like the liturgy which has been handed down from generation to generation.

Preaching is the heart of the worship service. Just like the heart, which supplies the blood to the whole body, preaching makes the Word of Christ accessible to the whole worshiping congregation. The worship service must, therefore, be understood in terms of an organic whole, where every part of the body is intimately connected to every other. When every part of the service is well coordinated and connected like the living body, preaching is alive and effective. When we compare preaching to the heart and the body to worship service, preaching is like the heart helping the blood reach every corner of the body through all the clear and interconnected arteries. Just as the heart is inseparable from the body, preaching is inseparable from the worship service. The unity of preaching and the worship service can be understood in the functional unity of prophet, priest, and pastor in the life of the church.[4] Preaching is preaching because of the worship service, and the worship service is alive because of preaching.

Preaching and the Order of Worship

An American friend told me that he was more comfortable attending a Korean church service than his own worship service. His church, one of the oldest and most prestigious churches in town, has become more liturgical by adapting aspects of the Anglican tradition into the worship service. However, the Korean church he attends combines Methodist, Presbyterian, Baptist, and Holiness church traditions, and has a simple liturgy and order of service, to which many Christians are accustomed. The order of worship in the Korean church, regardless of denominational affiliation within the Protestant tradition, is generally the same. The following order of worship is taken from a Korean church in New York City. This church, with more than three hundred members, is officially associated with the United Presbyterian Church in the USA:

> Silent Prayer and Praise (choir)
> Call to Worship
> Opening Hymn
> Responsive Reading
> Confession of Faith (Apostles' Creed)
> Prayer
> Hymn
> Scripture Reading
> Choir Anthem
> Sermon
> Prayer of Dedication
> Offering
> Offertory Prayer
> Congregational News
> Closing Hymn
> Benediction[5]

Although the order may differ slightly in each local church, there is no fundamental difference. For example, a Korean United Methodist Church in Boston or in New Jersey has an almost identical order of public worship.[6] Korean churches in this country have retained the same order of worship that was practiced in Korea. Chung Dong First Methodist Church in Seoul was the first Methodist church in Korea to be established by the first Methodist missionary, Henry Appenzeller, and is regarded as the most prestigious Methodist church in Korea. This church's worship service is generally considered the exemplar of Methodist church services in Korea. In June 1994, I attended the Sunday morning service and found the order of worship to be practically identical to that of the service of the Korean Presbyterian Church in New York City outlined above. The only difference was that the order of worship at the Chung Dong First Methodist Church in Korea is divided into four categories: Invitation to Worship, Confession, Sermon, and Dedication.

The order of a public worship service is like a chart that helps us see the path up the mountain. This chart was given to us many years ago by the first Protestant missionaries who came to Korea.[7] Very few changes have been made since then. In climbing up the Diamond mountain, our guide led us on a path which had been there for many hundreds of years, because it was safer for us to follow the same path that had been used by thousands and thousands of people. Likewise, most Korean Christians feel comfortable following a similar order of worship when they move to another church.

As we can see, the typical order of worship is centered on preaching, like most evangelical and free churches. "It is a sermon centered worship service."[8] However, what makes the order of worship in the Korean church different from most other American churches is the recitation of the Apostles' Creed, which is an essential element in worship. No service of worship is complete without it. Although there are many other creeds, including the Korean creed, the Apostles' Creed represents the orthodox view of the Korean church.

There is a growing interest in the Korean church in charting a new path to reach the pinnacle experience in worship. The path that leads the community of faith to a sacred experience in worship and preaching has "a memory, participating in a tradition reaching back across the centuries,"[9] but it also has hope, creating a new tradition reaching toward the future. Many young theological students seem more and more interested in developing a new order of worship using Korean cultural elements, especially the shamanic and Buddhist cultures, to provide a rich experience of worship. However, there is strong resistance to change, because the traditional Korean path feels both safe and comfortable. Charting a new path in the worship service takes time. In spite of resistance, change has begun to occur through experimental services led by young seminary students. The use of the shamanic mask dance, Pansori, and other traditional songs and rhythms in worship may one day begin gradually to influence the service of worship in the established church. Change will come when Koreans are willing to utilize our rich cultural resources to chart a new path for worship that is distinctive in our own tradition.

Although radical change is a slow process, one change that does not greatly alter the present order of worship in the Korean church is to simply eliminate the offertory and the announcements after the sermon, which occupy the apex of the service. When people are inspired by the witness to the Word, they should be allowed time to meditate and then to go directly out into the world for service. The offertory is often used as a substitute for service to the world. The offering should symbolically represent the fruits of one's service to the world. However, it is often used instead for the self-service of building big churches.[10] Moreover, Korean people, having been influenced by shamanism, believe that the more they offer at the altar, the more blessings they receive. This idea is contrary to the spirit of the Christian emphasis that the offering is not only directed to God but is also given without expecting to receive. Because of these misdirected ideas of offerings practiced in the service, it is best to eliminate the offertory as a significant part of the Sunday ritual. Moreover, the offertory interrupts the sacred moment of meditation after the sermon. Putting money in envelopes, filling out checks, passing plates, or having ushers walking through the aisles, destroys the solemnity of the worshiping spirit. Moreover, after the offertory is completed, the announcements immediately begin. As attention is directed toward the activities of the church, the congregation forgets what has been said in the sermon. The announcements disrupt meditation on the sermon and deprive members of the moment of sacrality. Cutting these two activities not only allows for the sacred moment of meditation following the sermon, but also eliminates ten or twenty minutes from the service. Since Korean worship usually lasts more than one and a half or even two hours, the elimination of the offertory and the announcements will shorten the worship service.

To replace the offertory, a wooden offering box could be placed at the entrance of each sanctuary. As people entered the sanctuary for the service, they could simply drop their offering in the box. This idea is in perfect harmony with Korean culture and with the biblical tradition. For example, in the Buddhist service, there is no offertory. The only offering Buddhists make is found in the symbolic act of burning incense as they enter the main hall. In my vision of the revised service, just as is practiced in Buddhism, the offering box would be located at the entrance to the church, so that people could offer upon entering or leaving whatever amount they could contribute. This is also biblically sound. In Mark 12:41-44, is the story of the poor widow who drops two small copper coins into the offering chest. Many Korean ministers think that replacing the offertory with the offering box will decrease the amount of offerings. However, in my experience, the amount of money collected in the offering box has been about the same as the amount placed in the offering plate.

Since church news and activities are printed in the bulletin, it is not necessary to spend time announcing them during the worship service. People who are interested in activities will read about them in the bulletin. Another option is to use the fellowship hour to remind people of activities that need to be stressed. Making announcements during the refreshment hour makes sense, because people who are interested in church activities generally remain for the social hour. And instead of the preacher announcing every activity, the laypeople who are responsible for specific activities can announce their upcoming programs. The announcement then becomes more than just an announcement; it initiates action as well. Dynamic interactions are possible when the announcements are made during the fellowship hour.

Many other aspects of the order of worship can be altered to give more meaning to the worship service, and to make preaching more effective in the life of the church. These changes would be beneficial not only to the Korean church but also to the American church.

In addition to the Sunday morning service, there are many other services in the life of the Korean church. In these services, the worship order is simpler and more informal, stressing the singing of gospel songs, prayers, and brief sermons.

Korean Preaching as an Extension of Prayer

Preaching is more than a simple witness to the Word or an exposition of scripture. It is a human response to the Word of God revealed through scripture, tradition, human experience, and nature. Because preaching is an expression of a human response to God and all creaturely existence, it is deeply rooted in meditation and reflective thinking in the divine presence. Mere intellectual and human imagination alone cannot make preaching truly prophetic and reflective of reality. It is necessary to reach into the depths of our spirituality. Thus prayers can serve as the background of preaching. In other words, preaching must be done prayerfully and in the mood of meditation. Prayers and preaching are inseparable. Preaching without a prayerful and meditative attitude may become a beautiful, sweet talk, but it cannot be authentic and prophetic preaching. The prayer life of the minister and the congregation is, therefore, the foundation of effective preaching. Perhaps the preacher's prayer life can be compared to the mindfulness in every step of climbing to the mountaintop, which symbolizes the apex of the sacred experience of preaching.

Perhaps one of the most distinctive characteristics of the Korean congregation is its prayer life. Since the beginning of our civilization, Korean people have learned that prayers are part of life. The indigenous religion of shamanism is intensely animistic, and its primary aim is to placate the spirits, which are regarded as not only more powerful than human beings but also in control of human destiny. Prayers are not only the most common but also the most effective means of appeasing the spirits. Since the spirits are everywhere, we have learned to pray everywhere we go. When we go home, we pray to the spirit of the home; when we go to the office, we pray to the spirit of the office; when we go to the mountains, we pray to the spirit of the mountains; when we go to the river, we pray to the spirit of the river. When we pray, we ask not only for the protection of the spirits but also for their blessings. When we build new buildings, when we start new businesses, or when we reach new stages of life, we pray to the spirits with offerings and rites. Buddhism also stresses meditation as the way of life. One of the cardinal doctrines of Buddhist living is mindfulness for all things. This mindfulness is expressed in prayer life. Thus, through traditional religions, the Korean people have been deeply grounded in the life of prayer.

Thus, praying without ceasing is a natural part of the Korean people. For Christians, prayers are directed not to the spirits but to God. When Korean Christians visit the home of friends, the first thing we do is to pray for the blessings and peace of that home. When we prepare to learn, for example, we pray before opening our books. Likewise, when we come to the church, the first thing we do is to pray. It does not matter whether the congregation is standing and singing the hymn or reciting the creed. The first thing a member does, as soon as the church is entered, is to sit down and pray for a few minutes before joining the worship service which is in progress.

In the Sunday worship service, one of the most important prayers is the congregational prayer, which replaces the pastoral prayer in the American church. This is, in fact, a laity prayer, because it is done by a lay leader, either a lay elder or deacon or deaconess in the church. I like to think of it as a layperson's "mini sermon," because it is more than a prayer in the ordinary sense. It usually lasts ten to fifteen minutes, and includes accounts from the story of Genesis to Revelation, and from the life of Abraham to that of Jesus. It is not only a prayer of personal witness and affirmation to the Christian faith but also a prayer of praise, thanksgiving, repentance, new life, petitions, and blessings. It always includes concerns and blessings for the minister and his or her family especially the spouse of the minister, the sermons to be preached, the choir members, especially the choir director, youth ministry, the youth director, volunteer workers, the members' livelihoods, and so on. Moreover, the prayer is said in a homiletic style, so that the tone is often so sharp and shrill that it is often difficult to think that this prayer is addressed to God on behalf of the congregation. There is, certainly, a similarity between preaching and prayer. Both of them are messages in God's presence. As Fred Craddock says, "Preaching is like prayer not only in the sense that God is the audience, but also in the sense that the message is the church's; it did not arrive in town with the pastor but was already there."[11] However, there is also a clear distinction between prayer and preaching. Prayer is directed to God on behalf of the congregation, while preaching is directed to the congregation in the presence of God. When this distinction is lost, prayer becomes preaching. My daughter, after attending a Korean worship service, asked, "Why did he shout to God when he prayed? Was God dumb or so old that he lost his hearing? I thought it was an insult to shout at him." Outsiders, who think that shouting in prayer insults God, misunderstand the intent, which is to demonstrate the petitioner's sincerity before God. Moreover, many Korean Christians have a misinformed notion of what constitutes prayer. They imagine that the longer they pray, the better the prayer is and the more blessings they will receive. Because of this mistaken belief, the prayer is extended with undue repetitions. Moreover, the congregational prayer is so spontaneous that repetitions are not easily avoidable. Often the prayer is so long and repetitious that it is difficult to concentrate on the prayer.

The congregational prayer is another area of the worship service that could be revised, changed from a prayer to prayers. Instead of a few lay leaders who take their turns praying, many laypeople could participate in the congregational prayers. A lay leader may initiate the prayers with praise and thanksgiving, or whatever he or she would like to say, and then other laypeople can offer prayers for their personal or congregational concerns, followed by the minister's brief prayer of recapitulation and assurance. Changing the congregational prayer to congregational prayers would allow more people to participate in the service, reduce boredom, and allow an opportunity for a pastoral prayer to express pastoral concerns. The change is imperative, because some lay leaders have used the congregational prayer as a shrewd forum to attack the pastor and his or her policies in the church. The change will be slow in coming because of many lay leaders' strong resistance, but it must occur in order to improve the public worship service.

Another distinctive form of prayer in the Korean congregation is known as a *Tong-sung Kido,* which means simultaneous loud prayers. Many different prayers in different voices create a strange feeling, which often reminds me of the simultaneous speaking of different tongues at Pentecost. Sometimes these prayers become intensely emotional and even become lamentations. In the *Tong-sung Kido,* people have a chance to resolve their *han,* which is the subconsciously seated anger of innocent suffering due to injustice. This psychological anger is deeply felt by Koreans who have been oppressed and have suffered under the injustice of racial discrimination in the United States.[12] This prayer gives them an occasion to let out their frustrations and anger. I like to think of this prayer as a Christian adaptation of shamanic *Han-puri.* This shamanic technique of resolving *han* is one of the most important functions of shamanic ritual, that of healing the psychological wounds caused by injustice. Instead of using the shamanic ritual, Korean Christians use

Tong-sung Kido as a means of resolving *han*. Although this prayer is still a part of the public worship service in many conservative churches, most Korean churches prefer to encourage this kind of prayer in less formal services, such as evening services or revival meetings.

Preaching as a Foreground of Music

In the Korean church, preaching and music are inseparable. Music is an essential element of public worship, because it animates and inspires people to hear the Word of God. Hymns and sacred music function in their own ways to convey the Word of God. Therefore, they represent an alternative form of witness to the Word. Most hymns are based on scriptural verses and are interpretations of them. If sermons are interpretations of and a witness to the Word, hymns are sermons in a different mode. Sermons and hymns diverge in their forms of delivery, but are essentially united together. When music is poor and the congregational singing loses its vigor, preaching also loses its effectiveness. Preaching and music support each other to make worship truly meaningful. In climbing up to the mountaintop, music is like the sound of water flowing from the top. It is the same water that surges from the top, but it creates many different sounds when it flows over rocks and into a stream. Just as the stream flows down from its source, music penetrates into the emotions of people so that they can fully experience the mountaintop of the preaching.

It is not only the prayer life but also the music that makes the Korean congregation distinctive. Korean people want and like to sing. From the beginning of our civilization, we have been known as a singing people. In fact, singing and dancing are a characteristic of Korean shamanism that distinguishes it from other forms of shamanism in Northeast Asia. For example, Siberian shamanism concentrates on sacrifice, while Japanese shamanism focuses on the ritualistic performance for the dead. Korean shamanism, however, tries to reach an emotional climax through singing and dancing.[13] Music and singing form the background of shamanic rituals. Shamans dance to the music and singing, in order to enter into the ecstatic state of meeting with gods and spirits. Shamans must learn how to sing, to chant, and to play musical instruments as preliminary steps to becoming full-fledged shamans. The shamans of Korea produced, throughout antiquity, musical instruments such as drums, *changgo* or long drums, small bells, gongs, and flutes.[14] The early shamanic tradition of singing and dancing became part of the Korean people. No entertainment seems to be complete without singing. When Korean people get together, we like to sing. Whenever we go to a party, we are asked to sing in front of guests. Even at concerts in Korea, the audience does not leave even a well-known stage singer to sing alone. They join him or her and sing along. Singing is a basic element of Korean culture. If we cannot sing, we cannot fully embrace our cultural life.

The music of the Korean people is also a part of their Christian life. Korean Christians want to sing hymns, especially gospel songs, and most carry their own hymnbooks. Since the hymnbook is standardized, it can be used in almost any church (i.e., Presbyterian, Methodist, Holiness, Baptist, and other denominational churches all use the same hymnbook). Because Koreans are expected to bring their own hymnbooks to church, few Korean churches provide hymnbooks for public worship services. Each member carries a hymnbook, because it is used not only in church but also at home, in Bible study groups, and during other occasions and activities.

During the worship service, hymn singing is stressed. As is the custom in many conservative churches, people usually gather for church about fifteen to twenty minutes prior to the service in order to sing their favorite hymns. Although the number of hymns is limited in the formal worship service, continual singing is stressed in informal services, such as evening services, prayer meetings, revival meetings, and other group meetings. Often more than half the meeting time is devoted to group singing. In addition to congregational singing, the Korean church stresses a good music program as a means of attracting people to the church.

Although most people come to a church to hear good preaching, the music program is a way to attract visitors who are less committed to the Christian faith. One of the most prosperous Korean churches in the New York area realized how important their music program was in drawing people to the church. During one of their public worship services, professional singers, most of whom were from the Juilliard School of Music, were the featured musicians. Another church invested a sizable amount of money in renovating their sound system and musical instruments simply because the members were interested in listening to and performing good music. A number of evangelists have noted that they can tell whether or not a church will grow simply by testing its sound system.

Korean Christians are particularly interested in singing familiar hymns and gospel songs, rather than in learning new hymns. This is why it is rare to find unfamiliar hymns being sung during the worship service. Many members are less interested in the content of the hymns, and more interested in the rhythm and movement of the spirit they experience while singing. In following the shamanistic motive, music and singing are used in the church to uplift human emotions, which open the congregation to the inspiration of the Holy Spirit.

One of the most constructive and innovative elements currently being used in a few Korean churches is ending the service each Sunday with a special hymn or song. Some church services use congregational favorites, such as "The Lord's Prayer" or "How Great Thou Art." One church that I often attend closes its worship service with this simple, yet inspiring song, which touches the hearts of many believers:

The good God,
The good God,
You are truly good,
Oh, my Lord.
Give us faith,
Give us hope,
Give us love,
Oh, my Lord.[15]

Korean Preaching and the Bible

No one can dispute the centrality and the uniqueness of the Bible in the preaching life of the church. "It is a primary obligation of the preacher to interpret Scripture,"[16] because it is the witness of the Word. If the Bible was canonized by and became the normative guide for the community of faith, then preaching must be biblical. Whether or not we adhere to the traditional categories of exegetical, textual, expository, thematic, and topical preaching, great attention should be given to the question, Does the sermon say and do what the biblical text says and does?[17] When preaching is not biblical, its authenticity is lost, for the Bible represents the norm of the Christian community. The church and the Bible, therefore, belong together. The Bible is the church's book, and the church is born of and nourished by the Word, which is witnessed in the Bible. Because of their mutual relationship, the Bible continues to be the only authoritative book for preaching and pastoral ministry.

The witness to the Word can be compared to the stream of water that flows from the mountaintop. Just as the road that leads up to the mountain is charted along the stream, preaching and the worship service are guided by the Bible. The importance of the Bible as the primary source of our understanding of the historical witness of Christ is undisputable for all Christians. And Korean Christians hold particularly fervent feelings about the Bible since it is deeply rooted

55

in the history of the Christian faith. The Bible has a unique place in the history of Korean Christianity, because Korean Christianity began with the Bible. More than two hundred years ago, two Korean scholars in China were converted to Roman Catholicism and returned to Korea with the Bible and other sacred relics of the Roman Catholic church. The Bible was translated into Korean and circulated among many people, who were later converted to Christianity. Even before the first Western missionary, Father Perre Maubant, arrived in Euiju city in December 1835, there were already Christians whose conversion had occurred from reading the Bible. By the end of the nineteenth century, most Christians in Korea had disappeared as a result of persecution. However, when the Protestant missionaries arrived they found that several Christians had survived and were still spreading the gospel through the Bible.[18]

Early Protestant missionaries in the late nineteenth and the early twentieth centuries were products of conservative and evangelical Christianity, which emphasized the centrality of the Bible in the church. Although missionaries were interested in helping the poor and the uneducated, their primary emphasis was placed on the study of the Bible. Translating the Bible into *Hangul* or Korean scripts was an important development in promoting Bible study groups. The success of Bible schools was enormous. Such schools grew from 45,000 in 1909 to 112,000 in 1934.[19] Later, the uniqueness of the Bible was reinforced by an ultraconservative fundamentalist group which dominated the theological trend of the Korean church. They believed in the inerrancy and verbal inspiration of the Bible, and were deeply influenced by the well-known fundamentalist, Gresham Machen, at Princeton Theological Seminary. Sun-joo Kil (1869–1935), the initiator of this fundamentalist movement, read the book of Revelation ten thousand times and 1 John 500 times. He interpreted the Bible through the Bible. He called this "self-hermeneutics."[20] It was Hyung-ryong Park (1897–) who eventually systematized Korean fundamentalism. The so-called self-hermeneutic, or interpreting the Bible through the Bible, became the distinctive earmark of ultraconservative fundamentalism, which includes the majority of Korean Christians.[21] Since these Christians believe not only in the inerrancy and the verbal inspiration of the Bible but also that God's revelation occurs in the Bible alone, they need no commentaries or other books to know God. Thus, most Korean Christians are people of a single book, the Bible.

The Bible symbolizes Christian identity for the Korean people. We can tell who the Christians are, because they carry their Bibles. Buddhists do not carry their scripture when they go to temples and shrines. Shamanic believers do not take a Bible along when they go to *kut* or shamanic rituals. Christians are the only people who carry their scripture when they go to church or another Christian meeting. One man told me that he can determine what kind of Christian a person is by looking at the Bible he or she carries. Christians who are well established and hold a high position in the church usually carry a big, leather-bound Bible. The people that carry old, leather-bound Bibles are considered more important persons in the church than those who carry new Bibles. The size and the age of the Bible signifies for many the relative position of a Christian within the church. "When you see someone who carries an old leather-bound Bible, you instantly know that he or she is an elder or deacon or deaconess in the church," he said. Some of what he says makes sense. Almost no one attends church without his or her own Bible. Coming to church without a Bible means that the person is either not an initiated Christian or is a visitor.

One Sunday at the last moment, I decided to attend a worship service in a Korean congregation away from home, so I did not have my Bible with me when I entered the church. When the scripture was read by a lay leader during the service, all members of the congregation read their own Bibles, following after him. Since I did not have my Bible, I decided to listen carefully to the reading of scripture by the leader. I raised my head and paid attention to his reading, as people usually do in an American church. Suddenly, an usher came toward me opening his Bible for me to read along with the leader. I was very embarrassed. In most instances the congregation reads the scripture aloud along with the leader. However, in some cases, the lay leader reads the entire scripture and the congregation follows along, silently marking the verses with a pen. This is the reason that everyone is expected to bring his or her Bible when attending church or other church-related meetings.

In addition, many preachers ask the congregation to open their Bibles and to read specific verses together. Even when the congregation has not been asked to read certain verses together, they always open their Bibles so as to meditate on key verses while listening to the sermon. For Korean Christians the sermon has to be biblical and exegetical. This type of propositional sermon is commonly used in the Korean church. Unlike other forms of interpreting biblical texts, in this exegetical sermon "a biblical text is treated line by line, or verse by verse, to explain its meaning and relevance for today."[22] This type of sermon was popular from the time of Cyprian until Karl Barth. The Korean church has become the present-day custodian of the traditional way of interpreting the biblical text through preaching. The Reformation principle of *sola scriptura* is not only the church's doctrine, but it is also frequently practiced. Literal biblicism with ultraconservative pietistic fundamentalism has become the foundation of the Korean church. Even though it may be false, there is a strength in this position because unwavering biblicism provides Christians a strong identity.[23] Although the idea of "one book alone" was imported to Korea, it proved to be a helpful doctrine for those of us who needed to cling to certitude in times of crisis and uncertainty. Even today, interest in studying the Bible outweighs all other topical studies in the Korean church. Generally a study group means a Bible study group. Moreover, church growth has been primarily attributable to Bible study. A new congregation often begins as a Bible study group at someone's home, lending credence to the notion that "the Bible is often the foundation of the church."

The downside is that the idea of "the Bible alone" and the so-called self-hermeneutic, or interpreting biblical texts through the Bible, has incapacitated the Korean preacher's ability to be prophetic about the injustices of the world, and makes him or her ineffectual in communicating the profound implications of the Word for a changing world. Today's crucial issues such as social justice, human rights, women's liberation, and so on, are almost completely missing from most Korean sermons. These shortcomings are discussed further in chapter 4.

The distinctive character of the worshiping community of Korean Christians can be summed up by three emphases: prayer life, musical interest, and ultra fundamentalistic biblicism. Both our prayer life and musical interest are deeply rooted in our traditional culture and religions, but our ultraconservative fundamentalistic biblicism came from the West and became a trademark of Korean Christianity. In the past these three distinctive emphases made Korean worship vital and added a spiritual dimension to preaching. Today it is apparent that the Korean church must be liberated from the ultraconservative fundamentalistic doctrine it adopted from the first Western missionaries.

Korean Preaching in Various Services

In other worship services, such as early morning prayer services, evening prayer meetings, revival meetings, home visitations, or Bible study groups, the three cardinal emphases culminate in the sermon. Prayers, singing, and scripture readings eventually lead the worshipers toward the climax of the occasion: the sermon. Although prayers establish a proper attitude toward God, singing provides emotional uplift, and scripture readings guide the will toward the truth, it is preaching that ultimately draws us together to witness the presence of Christ in the world.

Of the many types of meetings and services which are held in the Korean church, the two of particular interest are revival meetings and early morning prayers. Revival meetings, which were introduced by the early missionaries, are no doubt remnants of the late-nineteenth-century revival meetings of New England. They were institutionalized and then gradually shamanized in the Korean church and have become a distinctive element of Korean Christianity. As is the custom in a shamanic ritual, during revival meetings music and singing are used to lift the gathering's human emotions to ecstasy. The repetitive singing is emphasized by shrill instrumental music in the background, and hand-clapping and bodily movement are encouraged during the singing. The singing, instrumental music, and physical movements that occur during the revival are, as they are for Korean shamans, a means of entering a trance state. When the singing stops, prayers burst forth spontaneously, and because people are emotionally charged, their prayers resonate loudly. The "simultaneous loud prayers," or *Tong-sung Kido*, often change to lamentations, asking divine vengeance against those who have caused *han* or innocent suffering. Revival meetings often last until midnight and sometimes all night. The following eyewitness account vividly describes the amazing phenomenon of the "simultaneous loud prayers" at a revival meeting:

> So many began praying that Dr. Lee said, "If you want to pray like that, all pray," and the whole audience began to pray out loud all together. The effect was indescribable. No confusion, but a vast harmony of sound and spirit, a mingling together of souls moved by an irresistible impulse to prayer. It

sounded to me like the falling of many waters, an ocean of prayers beating against God's throne. . . . Over on one side, someone began to weep, and in a moment the whole congregation was weeping. . . . Man after man would rise, confess his sin, break down and weep, and then throw himself to the floor and beat the floor with his fists in a perfect agony of conviction. . . . And so the meeting went on until two o'clock a.m. with confession and weeping and praying.[24]

I recall a revival meeting that I attended in Chicago some time ago. The church had invited a well-known evangelist from Korea. He kept the congregation until two o'clock in the morning. Being a "shamanic" Christian evangelist, he was not only a good storyteller but also a fine entertainer. When he finished telling a story, he would sing a hymn and dance; then he would begin to narrate another story. Like a shaman, he sang and danced as he told stories of his own life and experience. Not all revival ministers are as talented as shamans. Most are ordinary preachers who talk about their personal witness during the revival meeting. However, the most important aspect of the revival meeting is the resolution of *han*, the suppressed feeling of resentment and anger against injustice.

Revival meetings have long been abused by preachers to benefit themselves financially. As we have noted, the revival meeting is fully institutionalized in the Korean church. Churches sponsor at least two revival meetings a year, with each meeting usually lasting two to three days. Guest preachers are invited to lead these meetings. Enormous amounts of money change hands during revival meetings. Since people are highly emotional during the meeting, they are vulnerable to offering more than they can actually afford to contribute. A friend who teaches in a theological seminary was invited to preach at a revival meeting in Los Angeles while attending another meeting in that city. The minister of the church offered him one thousand dollars for his service, but he refused to accept the money. He said, "The revival meeting was to exploit poor people who seek only their spiritual enrichment." There are many such unethical operations, sponsored by so-called successful preachers or prominent leaders, in progress in the Korean church. Sometimes, well-known evangelists from Korea are invited to come to America where they "harvest" tens of thousands of dollars at revival meetings. In return, they invite their Korean-American clergy friends back to Korea to do the same thing. Using ecclesiastic authority to attain personal benefits from poor and helpless people is one of the most grievous sins that can be committed by ministers of the gospel. Ridding the church of the calculated knavery of unethical leaders is one of the most urgent tasks and charges of the prophetic voices in our time.

Early Morning Prayer Meetings

The other service which is distinctively Korean in character is the early morning prayer meeting. While the revival meeting is deeply influenced by shamanism, the early morning prayer meeting is a Christian adaptation of a Buddhist practice. During a stay at a Buddhist retreat center in Korea, I was awakened at about four each morning by the monks, who would pass through the living quarters, beating their wooden hand bells. The huge temple bell then shattered the silent air, calling the faithful to the main hall for the early prayer meeting. As the monks chanted people entered the hall from various directions and offered incense to the Buddha. Then we sat quietly, following the order of the early morning worship.

This Buddhist tradition was adapted by the Christian church in Korea. It is often said that at one point Christians became so aggressive in this prayer practice, that they began to hold early morning prayer meetings even earlier than the

Buddhists. When I was a boy my mother would wake me before four in the morning so that we could attend the early morning prayer meeting. We had to use a square lantern to light the road leading to the church because it was too dark to see. Most people are not as ambitious as my mother and I were, so in most churches the morning prayer service does not usually start until five-thirty or six o'clock in the morning, and typically lasts about an hour. Even though these are called prayer meetings, they are actually informal worship services, which include singing, praying, scripture readings, and preaching.

Many Korean churches in America have given up holding early morning prayer meetings, because their members' lifestyles have changed drastically since coming to the United States. However, these prayer meetings seem to be experiencing a revival in some Korean churches in America. Many Koreans think, subconsciously perhaps, that the key to spiritual life is the early morning prayer service. When the church is not growing or seems to be spiritually weak, the preacher often begins holding early morning prayer meetings. Although few people may attend, many ministers believe it is still worthwhile to continue offering these services. My own belief is that the spiritual vitality of the Korean congregation may well depend on its commitment to attending prayer meetings before the start of daily activities. Whether it does or doesn't, for the most part morning prayer meetings have become unpopular and because of this may eventually slip into the history of the Korean church's life.

CHAPTER 4

DISTINCTIVE CHARACTERISTICS OF KOREAN PREACHING

In this chapter, let me elaborate on my vision of what preaching, especially Korean preaching, ought to be. Although preaching is a communication of the gospel to the congregation, it is a special form of communication that involves more than mere technique. Preaching is an art in itself. It is, therefore, different from communicating ideas through lectures or announcing events to the public on the evening news. Taking ideas from the scripture and relaying them to the congregation is not authentic preaching. The thing that makes preaching authentic and different from other forms of communication is the preacher's witness to the Word. The word "witness" implies more than an idea or ideas; it has to do with an experience which has become a part of oneself. My image of preaching, therefore, is more than just sharing ideas about God or about the teaching of Christianity; it is a sharing of oneself, which is embodied by the preacher's witness to the Word. Because preaching means to reveal oneself, the whole self, it is an art which is unique to each preacher's own nature and cannot be imitated or reproduced by anyone else. In fact, preaching cannot be mirrored even by the person doing the preaching, because it simply cannot be repeated. The effectiveness of a sermon is in its newness. Thus, "Some very good sermons are never preached a second time."[1] Moreover, anyone who is interested in the ideas of or in imitating others is not an authentic preacher. The preacher, no matter how skillful in imitating another's communication techniques, how many good ideas he or she takes from the scripture, how well informed about the personal, social, and cultural background of the congregation, or how articulately he or she merges text and context, cannot be authentic unless the embodied self is being disclosed and given to the congregation.

> Preaching, therefore, is more than expounding the Scriptures, more than telling the story of Jesus, more than explaining the meanings of our beliefs, more than persuading people to accept Christianity intellectually and morally, more than sharing insights and knowledge of the Christian faith, and more than prophesying God's will to mankind. What, then, is preaching? Preaching, to me, is to give myself to the people whom I serve; it is the offering of myself.[2]

Preaching is a disclosure of the true self, the self that is neither molded by the expectations of the congregation nor wrapped in ideals about what constitutes a good preacher.[3] It is presenting not the self that is abstracted but the embodied self, the self that embodies not only the text and context but also Christ and culture. Whatever is said while preaching, therefore, must come from the whole self.

Preaching is more than a living art in an ordinary sense; it is meditation reflecting the embodied self, which is also connected with other selves. Meditation connects individuals with others and with God. Meditation yokes the human and divine ("yoke" comes from the same etymological root as yoga, a Hindu discipline aimed at achieving spiritual insight and tranquillity). If preaching is a form of meditation, then through preaching the preacher enters into the congregation, and through preaching Christ enters into us all. When we are in Christ, and the congregation and the preacher become one, preaching becomes genuine. When all become one, the preacher is united with the congregation in the Word and the Word is incarnate among them. In this kind of preaching, the distance between the text (biblical) and the context, between the preacher and the congregation, is closed.[4] In this kind of preaching, Christ is incarnate not only in the preacher but also in the congregation, and thereby enlightens all our hearts and minds. Thus, everyone is able to experience Christ's authentic existence in the world. The role of authentic preaching, then, is to help others experience Christ's authentic life in the presence of God, who unites everyone.

It is easy for us to say what genuine preaching should be; it is far more difficult for us to practice it. Our actual preaching must be constantly tested against our ideals. As we examine the content and styles of Korean preaching, we must not forget that genuine preaching is also holistic. In other words, Korean preaching is not genuine unless it discloses the wholeness of being a Korean who embodies both witness to the incarnate Word and the heritage of Korean history and culture. A mere imitation of Western preaching style does not make an authentic Korean preacher. Korean preachers must present themselves as Koreans, for preaching means to disclose ourselves, our whole selves, to our congregations.

We are the products of our own history and culture: long years of humiliation and oppression by other nations, the emotional and physical scars caused by a civil war in the 1950s, the fear and insecurity of political and social unrest caused by the division between North and South, and the unquenchable thirst for religious fervor, are all a part of our heritage. In spite of our painful and tragic history, we have rich cultural resources which have forged in us the endurance that distinguishes Koreans from all other people. Without pretension or shame, we must preach Christ by presenting ourselves as the embodiments of that tragic history, as well as the embodiment of the splendid and tragic culture of our past. Korean preaching is distinctive not because Christ is different, but because Koreans are different.

When Koreanness is lacking in preaching, it is no longer Korean preaching. Thus, authentic preaching, which is alive and real to the Korean church, must include the heritage of Korean history and culture. Only against the backdrop of this heritage can we discern and evaluate the distinctive characteristics of Korean preaching.

Most Popular Sermons Are Uncritically Exegetical and Uncompromisingly Doctrinal

One of the most distinctive aspects of Korean preaching is the lack of criticism in the exegetical and doctrinal sermons which are most popular in the Korean church today. As we have said, the Bible and the Apostles' Creed are the most important elements of the worship experience for Korean Christians, who are not only "people of the Bible" but also people of the church's doctrine based on the Apostles' Creed. For them, doctrine is the canon of canons: It is the principle by which they interpret the Bible. Uncritical interpretation is *"the direct and uncritical transfer of the text to the listener.* This [means] reading a passage of Scripture and then treating it in the sermon as though it had been written with this audience in mind."[5] This method prohibits a historical, literary, or sociopolitical explanation of biblical witness to the Word. The underlying assumption of this uncritical method of interpretation by conservative Korean fundamentalists is that the doctrine cannot be altered by biblical authority. Because they believe that the church's doctrine represents the essence of the biblical messages in the Old and the New Testaments, any scriptural interpretations that are not in harmony with that doctrine are necessarily unorthodox and must be rejected. For example, the Korean church regards the virgin birth of Jesus as not only true but also scriptural, although different scriptural interpretations are possible. With this kind of background, the Korean congregation expects sermons to be uncompromisingly doctrinal and uncritically exegetical, and preachers reinforce the importance of conservative fundamentalism by preaching sermons that congregations expect to hear. That is why this type of sermon is favored in the Korean church.

Except for very few cases, most sermons preached in Korean churches in America are indeed uncritically exegetical. Although the biblical text might be used for liberating the life of the congregation, it is instead used to confirm their fundamentalistic faith and to confine them within a wall of fundamentalist doctrine. In addition to the expectation of the congregation, there is another reason for the lack of criticism in the sermons. Most Korean ministers are convinced that the church grows faster when they preach from the Bible. Since most Korean Christians are fundamentalists who believe that the Bible alone contains the truth, they will come to church only if the preacher offers an uncritical exegesis of the Bible. So-called liberal preachers right out of seminary soon discover that the failure of their ministry is related, directly or indirectly, both to their liberal orientation toward church doctrine, and to their lack of commitment to uncritical exegesis. The use of historical criticism in preaching, for example, makes suspect the preacher's commitment to the Christian faith in the eyes of many Korean congregations. Few churches in the New York area, which have either long historical roots in America or the creative leadership of committed preachers, have succeeded without a fundamentalistic approach to biblical exegesis in preaching. Most Korean churches cannot survive without the protection of the fundamentalist doctrines, which give a sense of security, even if it is a false security, to uprooted Korean immigrants.

One practical reason why Korean preachers may prefer uncritical exegesis in preaching is that they simply do not have the time to consult commentaries or other resources that are available for building a sound biblical foundation to preaching, which has moral and social implications. Because they preach in so many different services and attend a number of church meetings that consume much of their time each week, most Korean preachers are too busy to spend a great deal of time on the preparation of their sermon.

Most Korean churches do not use lectionaries. Korean preachers simply pick their favorite texts. An examination of the preaching in one of the fastest-growing Korean churches in my area illustrates how this uncritical exegesis functions in the Sunday morning service. The minister preaches like a Sunday school teacher. He goes through the text thoroughly from one verse to another.[6] The congregation is always asked to read the verse together before it is explained. If the verse is particularly important to the preacher, the congregation is asked to read it again and again, until everyone has just about memorized it. He speaks so forcefully that the people in the pews automatically follow his command. Many people underline verses that the preacher emphasizes. (In truth, they sideline them because the verses in a Korean Bible are written vertically, from top to bottom). The preacher is not interested in the historical and contextual importance of the passage, since the background of the passage he expounds is never explained. He is not interested in historical and biblical criticism at all. He attempts to prove the text through the use of other passages in the Bible. Thus, he is a typical Korean preacher who uses the so-called self-hermeneutic methodology, interpreting the Bible through the Bible.

However, this minister's interest in uncritical exegesis also serves purely as an allegorical interpretation through which he tries to convey the spiritual meaning of the text. "Historically, the allegorical method has enjoyed the prestige of rabbinic and early Christian use and was widely popular for sixteen centuries."[7] Origen used the allegorical approach to the Bible by assuming that every word in the Bible was pregnant with spiritual meaning, since the Bible was dictated by God.[8] Because of his allegorical and self-hermeneutic exegesis in preaching, the typical Korean pastor is interested in neither the context of his congregation nor the issues that they face in America. Because his interest is only in the spiritual meaning of the text, there is hardly any coherent theme to help integrate his message into the lives of the worshipers. Without a central theme, the allegorical interpretation goes on from verse to verse. It takes about forty minutes to finish the text, and then the preaching simply ends.

Why are people attracted to this kind of preaching? I believe the answer is their orientation to fundamentalism. There is, however, another reason. As I listened to this minister's preaching, I felt relieved of the burden of reasoning (mental work) and the worries of real life in the world. I am sure that other people felt the same. Forty minutes were enough for me to rest and flee from the struggles of life through the spiritualization of ordinary events. This kind of preaching certainly appeals to many Koreans who have a shamanic background, since shamanism too provides a temporary release from the worries of real life through the trance. By spiritualizing the biblical texts, the preacher can easily make himself or herself spiritually superior to the laity, and can eventually assume the guise of a shamanic figure in the minds of the congregants.

Authentic exegetical preaching cannot dismiss the context of the text or the contexts of the people who hear the sermon. A sermon which disembodies the text, and removes people from their own context, is often more harmful than helpful. Moreover, this kind of preaching is not biblical. Charles Rice, quoting Edmund Steimle, noted, "The sermon which starts in the Bible and stays in the Bible is not biblical."[9] This kind of preaching may draw people to the church, but it eventually incarcerates them in an unreal world. It is time for Korean preaching to make a transition from the deductive approach, which uses the lived experience of the congregation as an "ornament" useful for illustrating the text, to an inductive approach to preaching. "For inductive [preaching], the real, lived experience of those [who are] within the community of faith is essential to the formation of the sermon and, in conjunction with the text, provides the sermon's message."[10] Good exegetical preaching should take the listeners' context seriously, so that the text truly reveals the embodied Word and animates the real life of service.

Stresses on the Witness of the Holy Spirit

The theme about which most Korean preachers prefer to preach is the "witness of the Holy Spirit." Korean preachers are fascinated by the work of the Holy Spirit because of their background in shamanism, which is also a religion of spirits. Preaching is animated by the presence of the Spirit, while the Spirit is made conscious through preaching. Because preaching and the presence of the Spirit are inseparably related, a good sermon is spiritual both in style and in content. No matter how efficiently organized, thoughtfully interpreted, practically contextualized, or insightfully presented, a sermon is not a good sermon unless it is "filled with the Holy Spirit." According to the Korean mind-set, as long as the sermon is spiritual, all other ingredients are insignificant. For most Koreans, it is the power of the Holy Spirit that produces a good sermon. However, we cannot completely rely on the Spirit to accomplish the work that we, as preachers, should do. As Craddock says, "Believing in the Spirit does not cut our work in half. God's activity in the world does not reduce ours one iota. Any doctrine of the Holy Spirit that relieves me of my work and its responsibility is plainly false."[11]

In my preaching ministry, my congregation constantly challenged me to preach spiritually and to preach more on the witness of the Spirit. My interest in the life and teaching of Jesus was not spiritual enough for my congregation. In the fellowship hall after the service, the congregation was given a chance each week to talk about my preaching. On many occasions, they said that my preaching lacked spirituality, and they often wanted to discuss the meaning of spirituality. What do we mean by spiritual preaching or the spirituality of preaching? Since I have been deeply impressed by the Buddhist spirituality that is, of course, a part of my cultural heritage, I seek the presence of the Spirit in depth and the voice of the Spirit in calmness. Because most people in my congregation were shamanistically oriented, they were simply unable to discern the subtlety of the Spirit in my preaching.

From my own shamanistic heritage, I also believe in the importance of charismatic spirituality in preaching. It is easy for us as Koreans to relate the Spirit to the power of life or vitality, called *ki* (*ch'i* in Chinese).[12] The Spirit, like water that nourishes and vitalizes the living, is the foundation of the preaching which nurtures the life of the congregation. Preaching is to witness the Spirit, for "it is that very Spirit bearing witness with our spirit that we are children of God" (Rom. 8:16). Preaching began with the coming of the Spirit, as we read in the story of Pentecost. With the coming of the Spirit like the rush of a powerful wind, everyone began to speak in other languages (Acts 2:1-4). What is important in this passage is not the ability to speak in tongues or to experience ecstasy, but the power to witness the presence of God. That is precisely why Peter's first sermon begins with the coming of the Spirit in the words of the prophet Joel:

> In the last days it will be, God declares,
> that I will pour out my Spirit upon all flesh,
>   and your sons and your daughters shall prophesy,
> and your young men shall see visions,
>   and your old men shall dream dreams. (Acts 2:17)

The Spirit that gave Peter the ability to preach also became the power for other disciples to preach their witness to Christ. Being deeply biblical in orientation, charismatic preachers typically raise their arms high above their heads, to receive the Spirit, and then, by directing their arms toward the congregation, "give" the Spirit. However, this gesture suggests more than Peter's perception of or Joel's thoughts of the Spirit. As we will discuss in chapter 5, there is a deep cultural implication for Koreans in one's attempt to divinize oneself to gain spiritual power, as the shamanic tradition explicitly demonstrates.

I am convinced, like many other Korean preachers, that the witness of the Spirit should be of central importance in preaching. The lack of spiritual emphasis is symptomatic of most preaching in the mainline American churches today. However, the proper understanding of the Spirit in preaching is more important than a mere emphasis on it. The danger that I feel is that undue emphasis on the Spirit in Korean preaching causes people to seek such things as miracles, ecstasy, personal power, and wealth, instead of the power of Christian witness and prophecy. This kind of misdirected emphasis (which, incidentally, was also common in the early church, as Paul pointed out to the Corinthian community) is rampant in Korean preaching because of Korea's roots in the shamanistic tradition. Shamans exercise the power of the spirits to heal the sick, to offer (and to acquire) personal success and prosperity, and to experience ecstasy. Like shamans, many Korean preachers think unconsciously that they can do the same through the power of the Christian spirit or the Holy Spirit.

This kind of temptation is common when one's church begins to decline. It is believed that one of the easiest ways to remedy the problems of a declining congregation is to seek spiritual power. Several years ago a young and well-educated minister of a Korean Methodist church in Chicago consulted with me following a continuing education class for ministers, which I taught at Garrett-Evangelical Theological Seminary. After being urged by his ministerial colleagues the young pastor had invited a well-known charismatic preacher from California to his church. This preacher possessed the gifts of speaking in tongues and healing. When his sermon reached its climax, he no longer spoke in an ordinary language, but shouted with a loud voice and then began to speak in tongues. The congregation had been deeply impressed by the preacher, and had learned how to speak in tongues. The young minister said, "Our church has been transformed. Everybody wants to speak in tongues. The budget of our church has doubled, and people have started to be active in the church again." I responded, "It is dangerous. You are leading your people astray. It sounds good, but it is temporary. Hear Paul's advice in 1 Corinthians 13! Stress love, which excels all other spiritual gifts."

Many people seek ecstasy to escape the reality of a hard life and mundane experiences. The temptation for many preachers is to preach a sermon that arouses the ecstatic experience of their people in the church. Preachers, however, cannot compete with shamans, who specialize in ecstasy.[13] The primary purpose of preaching should not be to aim at the experience of ecstasy, which can easily addict people to life in an unrealistic world. When the experience of ecstasy becomes an end in itself, preaching isolates people from the real world and encourages them to seek false emotional security in the psychic world. This is as destructive as the drugs that addict people on the street. Good preaching that emphasizes the witness of the Spirit must encourage people to engage the real issues which they confront in their lives, and to nurture them as truly loving and caring persons, enabling them to transform the world.

Conversion and Commitment

Even after more than a hundred years of Protestant mission in Korea and in the Korean American community, the nineteenth-century missionary emphasis on conversion and exclusive commitment to Christ has not altered. Conversion was emphasized in the early days, because Christianity was introduced to Korea where so-called heathen religions predominated. In order to win over those who had been affiliated with heathenish religious traditions, an exclusive commitment to Christianity was stressed. Emphasis on conversion is inherently exclusive and belongs to almost all religions in their initial stage. We see the exclusivism of Christianity in its beginning. Jesus said, "No one can serve two masters; for a slave will either hate the one and love the other, or be devoted to the one and despise the other. You cannot serve God and wealth" (Matt. 6:24). The favorite text for preaching on conversion is the story of Nicodemus (John 3:1-21). Among many popular passages, the text that has received more attention than any other is: "I am the way, and the truth, and the life. No one comes to the Father except through me" (John 14:6). This kind of exclusive commitment to Christ was necessary in the early church and is still important to those Korean preachers who are biblically and dogmatically evangelical and fundamentalistic.

When I served as a preacher in a Korean congregation, it was almost impossible to dismiss the importance of conversion and exclusive commitment to Christ. One Sunday morning I preached on the Ten Commandments from Exodus 20:1-17. I expounded the first one extensively: "You shall have no other gods before me" (Exod. 20:3). After the service, I noticed one of the women from the nearby Air Base weeping. Before I could ask about what had made her cry, she ran out of the building. Later, I was told that the woman still had a small Buddhist altar in her house. She did return to church for a few Sundays, and I had almost forgotten about her until one Sunday she asked me to come to her house to destroy the Buddhist altar. I was initially shocked and did not know how to respond to her request. However, several other members knew what needed to be done to destroy it.

That evening I was escorted by these members to the woman's house, where I found a small altar, like the small

Shinto box that my family maintained in our house during the Japanese occupation. The woman was afraid to touch any items in the altar. The others in attendance asked me to take the relics out of the altar. As I did so, I discovered that the altar belonged to the Nichiren sect of Buddhism, an indigenous Japanese Buddhist sect. I was then given a hammer and asked to destroy the jar and other items from the altar. We burned charm papers in front of the troubled woman, and sang "Onward Christian Soldiers." I said a few words of comfort to the woman, followed by a prayer for our exclusive commitment to Christ. When this brief ceremony was over, the woman loudly proclaimed, "I am free, free from the Buddhist spirit. I now belong to Christ." For the first time I saw the radiance shining from her face.

My great-grandmother's experience of almost a hundred years ago had been repeated here in my Korean congregation in America. After what happened to the woman from the Air Base, I realized how influential it had been for me to preach on an exclusive and personal commitment to Christ. The very act of destroying the altar was my preaching, for preaching is more than verbal communication. It is an act of presenting the real self, the whole embodied self, to the faithful. Everything I did during the brief ceremony at the woman's house was my preaching on conversion and exclusive commitment to Christ. I am still ambivalent about the event of destroying the altar as a means of preaching exclusive commitment to Christ. Symbolically and psychologically it was helpful to the woman, who felt she had to choose between Christianity and Buddhism. I could justify the act biblically from a fundamentalistic perspective. However, in today's pluralistic and multicultural context, my act was questionable. Is it right to continue to preach exclusivism and to encourage other ministers to preach the same?

It is this exclusive claim of Christianity that makes us, Korean Christians, the orphans of our own culture. By becoming Christians, we are taught we must reject shamanism,

Buddhism, Confucianism, and other traditional beliefs, which are the foundations of our cultural heritage. Moreover, exclusivism is incompatible with the concept of a pluralistic society. My suggestion, then, is to preach conversion and *total* commitment to the Christian faith without exclusivism. In other words, our preaching should aim at our complete commitment, with openness to other faiths. Our commitment to the Christian faith must be both strong enough and generous enough to include the other religious traditions, which are a part of our heritage. This approach to preaching seems to me to be faithful not only to the scriptures but also to the context of today's pluralistic world.

Reflection on the Korean Context: Suffering and Nationalism

The common ethos that unites the Korean people is the experience of suffering. Historically, we suffered collectively and individually for many generations under the domination of our neighboring countries, China and Japan. The Second World War left Korea free of dominance by Japan but internally divided between North and South. The scar of our civil war in the early 1950s reminds us that our suffering is not over. After a persistent struggle for justice and democracy, which has lasted for decades, Korea still suffers the division that has already lasted half a century. Koreans, therefore, believe themselves to be a *han*-ridden people, a people whose deep psychological wound has become their collective unconscious.

It is, therefore, natural that the suffering of Christ draws and sustains us as Korean Christians. Christianity, for us, is the religion of suffering that overcomes our suffering; it is the power of Christ's suffering that heals our wound. This healing power of Christ's suffering is the central message of Korean Christianity, and distinguishes it from the religions of our heritage. Although Buddhism comforts us to some degree, because it teaches that suffering is inescapable in life, for Buddhism suffering is an existential problem. To exist means to suffer: Suffering and existence are one in two different appearances. Buddhism offered a philosophy that explained the inevitability of our suffering, but it failed to really address the ethos of our people, because it stressed detachment from the world.

On the other hand, Christianity provides us with the concept of dynamic and participatory suffering, which gives us meaning and hope that we can transcend suffering through the suffering of Christ. Thus, the most meaningful and healing message that we, as Christian preachers, can convey to our suffering congregations is the suffering Christ. In the message of wounded suffering, both Christ and the Korean people, the text and the context, become one and incarnate in the church, which gives us meaning and hope. During the Easter season, while Western Christians focus on the resurrected Christ, Korean Christians identify closely with the suffering and crucified Christ. People in my congregation always said that the resurrection means the end. "It's all over!" they would say when Easter finally arrived. In other words, celebrating Easter Day in the Korean church means a closing ceremony. On the other hand, for most American Christians, the resurrection means the beginning of new life. Because Koreans see Easter from the perspective of the suffering and death of Christ, resurrection marks the end rather than the beginning. The suffering and tragedy of Christ are so closely identified with the Korean people that the cross is a central theme in Korean preaching.

If the ethos of Koreans is closely identified with suffering, the idea of "the suffering servant" in Second Isaiah is also closely connected with Korean nationalism. Suffering and oppressed people often look for their identity within the construct of divine purpose in the world, as the people of Israel have done. Moreover, the unprecedented expansion of

Christianity in Korea has led Korean Christians to think of themselves as the chosen people, chosen to witness the suffering Christ in the world. The general perception of Korea as the "new Israel" is well described by Harold Hong, former president of the Methodist Theological Seminary in Seoul:

> It would be unfair to say that the Korean people were more receptive and responsive to the Christian gospel than any other nation in Asia. But we strongly believe that we are now the chosen people of God and that we are under the special providence of God. This strong faith has actually made the Korean church the most rapidly growing church in the world.[14]

Preaching on suffering and nationalism certainly reflects the ethos of the Korean people. Identifying our suffering with the suffering of Christ and overcoming our suffering through our fellowship with Christ are important concepts that Korean preaching has developed.[15] However, Korean preaching should attempt to do more than meet the psychological and spiritual needs of our congregations in America. It must also reflect realistic solutions for suffering, and provide specific guidelines for action to eliminate injustice. Korean preaching should balance its emphasis between Christ as sufferer and Christ as liberator. Thus, our great challenge is to take a liberationist perspective in our preaching to counterbalance the conservative, fundamentalist perspective that has dominated the Korean pulpit for so long.

Koreans in America not only celebrate every important Korean national holiday, but also expect to hear its significance from the pulpit. For most of us, our nationalism is closely connected to nostalgia for our motherland. As strangers in a foreign land, we look for the meaning of our existence in doing something worthy for our motherland. Thus, one of the most popular themes in Korean preaching is the reunification of South and North Korea.

Although nationalism is a glue that unites the Koreans in America, preaching on nationalism has an inherent danger. It can easily foster ethnocentrism and a false pride that eventually erodes the universality of Christian love. Prior to 1945, the central message from the pulpit was about freeing Korea from Japanese rule. Now the Korean church in America is an immigrant church. It is time for us to challenge our congregations to transcend nationalism and to search for our identity as Korean Americans.

Emphasis on "This" World's Blessings and the "Other" World's (Heavenly) Rewards

Most of us, whether we are Americans or Asians, want to receive blessings not only in this world but also in the heavenly world. However, these two types of blessings sometimes seem to contrast with each other. As biblical fundamentalists, it seems natural for most Korean preachers to think that the poor and unfortunate will be rewarded in heaven, while the rich and fortunate will be punished in hell. This idea is clearly expressed in Jesus' Sermon on the Mount and other teachings. However, paradoxically, most Koreans believe that both the poor and the rich are rewarded in heaven. They understand the blessings of this world in terms of personal and material rewards rather than social justice and ethical living; and they perceive heavenly blessings as spiritual manifestations of worldly blessings. This kind of interpretation comes from the Korean culture, especially from shamanic thinking.

"You don't preach on blessings," my congregation often said to me. I thought I did. "Didn't I preach on the blessings of joy, peace, goodness, and love?" I responded. They replied, "We mean the real blessings, the *bok*, you know." They came to church to receive the *bok*, which meant wealth, success, health, longevity, and having many children at home. They want to have the *bok* now, but they also want to have it in its spiritual form in heaven. They told me that our church was not growing fast enough, because I did not preach on the *bok* or the material blessings of this world. Most growing Korean churches' central message deals with the *bok*. For example, Paul Yonggi Cho, who boasts that his church has the world's largest congregation, nearly half a million members, promises the *bok* in his preaching, which satisfies people's appetite for material blessings. He said,

> The preacher is like a gourmet cook. . . . There are many hungry people in the world. If the preacher prepares a delicious meal on the table, people will naturally be attracted to come to it. Thus how we prepare our gourmet meal to satisfy the appetite of the people will determine our success in ministry.[16]

Some think that the emphasis on material blessings is based on a naive adaptation by the church of modern materialism.[17] However, this kind of thinking is actually deeply rooted in Korean shamanism. People go to shamans to receive the *bok* from their ancestral spirits. They come to church for the same reason. Korean shamans always say, "The more you give to the spirit, the more you receive." The same kind of message is heard from the pulpit. Although it is unfair to conclude that preachers of all growing Korean churches promise material blessings in this life, I have seen enough evidence of it that it concerns me greatly. I do not believe that this kind of preaching is distinctly Korean. Many television evangelists and other preachers in the United States who stress positive thinking also practice this kind of preaching. I think that good preaching should be based on critical reflection of the Bible and sound theological interpretation. Using the Bible as a proof text to support one's own interests may have unfortunate consequences. When preaching loses its prophetic dimension and yields to human greed, it becomes no more than a sales pitch.

No one takes preaching seriously unless the promise of heavenly rewards is included in the message. The promise of worldly blessings must be balanced with that of heavenly rewards. Korean preaching in the early days stressed the promise of heavenly rewards to comfort the suffering and oppressed: Their suffering on earth would be compensated in heaven. Those who were poor in this world would be rich in heaven if they became Christians. Thus, conversion was the key to receiving eternal blessings. Although in most Korean churches, the content of preaching has shifted its emphasis from heavenly rewards to this world's blessings, the promise of heavenly rewards is still one of the most prominent topics preached in many poor Korean American communities. Since most of my congregation in North Dakota consisted of the Korean wives of U.S. servicemen, not an affluent community, their comfort came from hearing that Jesus had prepared a place for them in heaven.

Koreans have a tendency to think that there is continuity between earthly blessings and heavenly rewards. Because we believe that the blessings in this life stem from our faith in Christ, we believe that we will also be blessed in heaven. If faith makes us wealthy in this life, then the same faith must also make us wealthy in heaven. By this logic, the more blessings we have in this world, the more heavenly blessings we will receive, for both forms of blessings derive from our faith. The heavenly realm is simply an extension of this world. Obviously, this kind of thinking is deeply influenced by the shamanic worldview, where matter is interchangeable with spirit. The more spiritual we are, the more material we can possess, and vice versa. Because of the continuity between the spiritual world and this world, when powerful heroes and great officials die, they become powerful and influential spirits in the spiritual world. This shamanistic idea is so deeply embedded in the Korean mind-set that it allows the perpetuation of injustice and discourages the reform and renewal of society. Korean preaching, following this shamanistic idea, stresses propositional faith and cheap grace, which appeases and supports the wishes of the wealthy and powerful people in the church. It is time for Korean preaching to renew its emphasis on the living faith, which offers justice for all people.

Use of Rich Cultural Imagination, Stories, Symbols, and Aphorisms

Korean preaching is truly distinct from other preaching because of its use of Korean cultural images to illustrate sermons. The most creative cultural imagination of Koreans comes from the Korean language itself. Language is one of the most complex but refined forms of cultural expression, conveying the many subtleties of human emotion and cognition. Because language is the primary tool of communication, the effectiveness of preaching depends largely upon the appropriate and constructive use of language. Obviously, preaching in Korean for the Korean congregation is not only most effectual, but also most meaningful. For those Koreans who live outside Korea, hearing sermons spoken in their native language is a liberating experience. In the marketplace or in the workplace, they must communicate in English, their "second" language. This both limits their capacity to express their needs and wishes, and frustrates them. When they come to church, however, they can freely converse with one another, sing hymns together, and hear sermons in their native language without constraint. In this respect, the Korean language is not only an effective tool of communication but a means of liberating Koreans from the emotional exhaustion of their diasporic existence. It is also liberating for us, as Korean preachers, to be able to use our native language in preaching. No matter how well we learn to speak and write in English, we cannot master the English language unless we are fully acculturated in American culture. Many subtle American expressions, particularly American humor, jokes, and wit, are difficult for nonnative speakers to understand. When I was serving an English-speaking congregation soon after finishing my seminary education, I spent many hours each week preparing a sermon in English. When I preached the first sermon, a lay leader of my congregation encouraged me by saying, "Don't worry. We know what you were trying to say." Preaching in English was and still is a painful experience for me.

One of the elements that makes Korean preaching special and unique is the use of the Korean language. When the Korean language service is replaced by an English language service, the Korean church will never be the same. A new character of preaching and distinctive form of service will emerge as the Korean church makes the transition from a Korean-speaking congregation to a second-generation, English-speaking congregation.

Traditional Korean folktales and stories are rich resources that can illuminate biblical texts and illustrate sermons. However, the storytelling method is rarely used in Korean preaching, except for a few minjung theologians who use folktales to illustrate the oppressiveness of minjung experience.[18] Since Korean preaching as a whole uses a deductive approach deeply rooted in evangelical fundamentalistic biblicism, stories are only used as ornaments to illustrate exegetical themes.[19] However, the biblical themes of suffering and innocent sacrifice can be illustrated by Korean folktales as well. For example, the story of Chunhyang (Spring Fragrance) tells of a beautiful woman from a poor family. Chunhyang, who refused to yield to the lust of a tyrannical magistrate, was beaten, imprisoned, and sentenced to be publicly hanged. The story ends with retribution and restoration of justice. The story of Simchung, the young daughter of a blind man, is also well known to most Korean people. A

Buddhist monk told Simchung's father that he would recover his vision if he could donate three hundred bags of rice to a Buddhist temple. Hearing this, Simchung sold her life for three hundred bags of rice to some rich Nankin sailors who were looking for a maiden to sacrifice to sea monsters during their journey on the high seas. Although the story has a happy ending, it expresses the common experience of the oppression of the poor and helpless. These two stories are excellent backgrounds for preaching, for example, the liberation of Korean women and the poor in the church.

The story of the Emileh bell, one of the treasures of ancient Silla, tells us about the sacrifice of innocence, of beauty, and of pain. The story says that a huge temple bell was cast of the best metal purchased with people's donations. But the bell did not ring correctly, even when struck by the strongest man. In order to recast the bell, more donations were collected. Among the donors was a woman who was too poor to offer anything but her own baby. The baby was thrown into the molten metal and the bell was then recast. When the bell was struck, it produced the perfect and magnificent sound of the baby's cry. The bell continues even today to reproduce the voice of the noble little soul, crying "Emileh" (Mama), rather like Jesus' cry from the cross, "Abba" (Daddy).

Another story that deals with sacrifice and innocent suffering tells of Pali-congju, the rejected seventh princess. According to this story, the king had no son but only daughters. When the seventh daughter was born, he was so angry that he put her in a stone box and cast it into the sea. However, she was saved by the dragon king. Soon her father became ill because of his sinful act. Only the medicine water in the Western sky could cure him. But all six of his other daughters, whom he had raised in his house, refused to go to the Western sky, because it was too dangerous. However, when the rejected princess heard of it, she volunteered to go to the Western sky. After long years of suffering and hardship, she returned with the medicine water and revived her father, who had died. This is one of the most popular stories told by shamans in our time.[20] Many stories like these could be used to illustrate the sacrifice, suffering, and death of Jesus.

However, I have not found any Korean preachers who use these or other such traditional Korean stories to illuminate biblical texts or to illustrate their sermons. Instead, they use stories that come from Western sources. They draw upon Greek mythologies but never Asian or Korean legends. The reason is conspicuous. Because the Christian faith that Koreans have adopted is exclusive, any old stories or legends having their origins in early traditional religions cannot be appropriated in their preaching. Even though preachers may be interested in Korean folklore, they are afraid to use it in preaching. The very mention of the words "Buddhism" or "shamanism" in the pulpit is offensive to most people in the Korean church.

A personal experience may help to show the risk, as well as the opportunity, of using stories from other religious traditions for sermon illustrations. Several years ago, as a guest preacher, I spoke on the topic "the prodigal son," using the text from Luke 15:11-32. I used a similar story from Buddhism to illustrate the theme. In the Buddhist story, the father goes out to find the son and get to know him as a friend. The father brings him home and adopts him.[21] The Buddhist story illustrates a different dimension of love as found in Asian spirituality. The next day I was accused of being a Buddhist preacher. That church never again invited me to speak. However, when I was invited by another church to deliver the sermon on Father's Day, I decided to preach on the same topic, using the same text, with the same story for illustration. This time I mentioned not a word about Buddhism. When I greeted the congregation at the front door after the service, they told me they thought that it was a wonderful story, one that perfectly illustrated the Father's love. Moreover, they seemed to appreciate their own cultural tradition, knowing that they as Asians had a traditional story similar to the parable in the Bible. I hope that they discover someday that the story I told them has its origin in Buddhism, and that they thereby come to appreciate religious traditions other than their own. We need gradually to incorporate Korean cultural elements into our preaching through stories. At this point, we need not, and perhaps should not, refer to other religions. Until we feel that our congregations are ready to accept other religions as part of the Korean heritage, we must avoid in our preaching utilizing religious symbols that may become stumbling blocks for our faith.

Life stories are also powerful preaching tools when they are properly appropriated. In almost all Korean preaching, however, I have discovered that most life stories are taken from the West. I have heard few life stories about historic Korean figures, even though countless stories from the Western world are used to illustrate Korean sermons. When I went to hear one of the most respected Korean preachers, a man who is well informed in Korean literature, I had expected to hear sermons based on the life stories of well-known Koreans. However, I was disappointed because his sermons were illustrated with the life stories of Western people such as Thomas Kepler, Pablo Casals, Samuel Leibowitz, Horatio Nelson, Winston Churchill, Dwight Moody, Francis Parkman, Julio Iglesias, Dorothy Day, and others, and actors, scientists, theologians, politicians, and ordinary persons. Why not also use the stories of well-known Korean actors, scientists, scholars, and sages to illuminate biblical themes and to illustrate his preaching? It is important to make a conscious effort to incorporate the life stories of Korean figures as much as possible into Korean preaching so that it becomes truly indigenous and accountable to the Korean cultural context. My suspicion is that most Korean preachers use sermon preparation materials which are written in English when they prepare their sermons. We need to do some homework to find more illustrative materials from Korean cultural resources.

The use of symbols in preaching also comes from the cultural imagination. Most Korean preachers use biblical symbols in preaching because of their strong emphasis on uncritical exegesis. However, there are creative ways to use cultural symbols in our preaching. Some of the symbols which are genuinely meaningful to Korean people deal with ordinary life experience. For example, the bamboo tree, which seems to depict the ethos of Asian people, can readily be incorporated in preaching because the bamboo's inside is hollow, and is clearly a symbol of Christ's emptying himself in incarnation.[22] In the same way, the empty *ondol* floor, which is heated from below, implies the same meaning. Water and wind have special meaning for Asian people and signify spontaneity and interpenetration, which are functions of the Spirit. The symbol of *taeguk*, or the great ultimate balance, consists of yin and yang. Yin (female, darkness, etc.) and yang (male, light, etc.) are opposite but united. This symbol helps illustrate the two natures of Christ or the inseparable relationship existing between divine immanence and transcendence. There are many other symbols which not only reflect distinctive characteristics of Korean culture but also illuminate living the experience of the Christian faith. The effective use of symbols that opens us to new awareness of our context and consciousness is the key to good preaching.

Finally, I would like to recommend the use of Korean aphorisms and proverbs to illustrate Korean sermons. Aphorisms and proverbs are folk wisdom grown out of the everyday experiences of the common people in Korea. Most Korean proverbs initially existed only orally and were not written down until much later. I have used many such proverbs to illustrate sermons. For example, to illustrate the power of yielding, I would say: "If you hate him, give him one more ricecake." (Ricecake was regarded as a precious food in early days.) This saying means that we should be nicer to the person we hate, which is similar to Jesus saying, "If anyone forces you to go one mile, go also the second mile." By doing more than what the enemy wants, we allow the enemy to repent and to become our friend.[23] Other Korean sayings I have used in sermons are: "The land where you live is your native country," which is used to illustrate our immigrant life in America. "It takes the clap of both hands to make a sound" is used to illustrate harmony and cooperation in Christian life. "It is darkest right under the lamp" helps to illustrate how Jesus was not accepted in his own town but was accepted by people far away.[24] These sayings are capsules of wisdom, which carry spiritual, moral, and practical implications for living. If we want to make sermons practical to the lives of common people, we can find an important place for aphorisms or proverbs in sermon preparation.

Use of Mannerism and Tone

As I said earlier, Koreans become spontaneous and very emotional in informal services, such as evening services, Bible study groups, or revival meetings. However, they are more restrained and reserved when they come to the public services on Sunday. In informal services, they exhibit their shamanistic ethos; in the formal service, they become more Confucian in their conduct. Let me briefly comment on the styles of delivery in the Sunday service.

Koreans, as a rule, are quite reserved, and our decorum plays an important role, because the Confucian notion of propriety has long been a part of our public life. Korean preachers are quite sophisticated and behave modestly in preaching (although there are exceptions, such as those who belong to free church traditions or radically fundamentalistic groups such as the Full Gospel church). Korean preaching as a whole is not really different from that of most American preachers in the mainline church. What seems to make Korean preaching distinctive is the use of tones. Many Korean preachers have a tendency to "shout and yell" with a high-pitched tone. Shouting has a symbolic meaning in preaching. Fred Craddock says, "The Word of God *at the ear* is a whisper; *at the mouth* it is a shout."[25] The Word is symbolically heard as a whisper and spoken as a shout. Shouting should not, therefore, be taken literally. It means that the message we speak to the congregation is urgent and important.[26] Nevertheless, many first-generation Korean American ministers not only actually shout but also yell in their preaching.

When my children first attended a Sunday morning service in the Korean church, they were frightened by the sermon. They did not want the preacher to shout and yell at them. They also thought that it was indecent for the preacher to behave like an uncivilized person in a solemn ceremony like the church service. Strangely enough, most first-generation Korean Americans like to hear shouting and screaming from the preacher. In fact, the churches of shouting preachers seem to grow faster than those of reserved preachers. I personally dislike the shouting-and-yelling sermon, but I suppose it is a matter of personal taste. The current trend of Korean preaching seems to be more reposed and less authoritarian in tone. Also, many congregations no longer respond with "amens" or "hallelujahs" during the public worship service. Culturally, Korean preaching is changing from the shamanic to the Confucian style of delivery. As Koreans become more Americanized, the style of Korean preaching will change in order to accommodate the new needs of the Korean people in America. I cannot say how much Korean preaching will retain its Korean distinctiveness as Koreans become more Americanized. I can only hope that the positive aspects of Korean preaching will remain, whatever the form Korean preaching takes in the future.

Finally, let me emphasize again that Korean preaching must gradually change from a deductive and propositional approach to an inductive and contextual approach. The deductive approach assumes the universal validity of the biblical text regardless of different human living situations. This approach creates a deep gulf between the text and the reality of Korean life. This approach in preaching, since deeply grounded in evangelical and fundamentalistic biblicism, not only prohibits any critical, historical, or sociological understanding of the Bible, but also further alienates the Korean people from their own culture and history, and the sociopolitical conditions in which they live. An inductive approach, on the other hand, liberates them from the confinement of rigid biblicism and helps them participate in their history, culture, ethos, and their existential experience. When the biblical text is interpreted in light of the living experience of the Korean people, who embody their cultural traditions and their future predicaments, Korean preaching is not only alive but also nurtures the living faith, faith that is accountable to the reality of the world in which the congregation lives. In this kind of preaching, the listeners (the Korean congregation), the text (biblical witness), and the preacher (proclamation) are united. Thus the gulf between the biblical text and the human context, as well as that between Christ and culture, is closed, allowing a distinctive indigenous form of Korean preaching to emerge in the future.

CHAPTER 5

THE AUTHORITY OF THE KOREAN PREACHER

The authority of the preacher seems to be correlated with the effectiveness of his or her preaching. According to the gospel, people were "astounded at [Jesus'] teaching, for he taught them as one having authority, and not as the scribes" (Mark 1:22). Here, authority does not simply come along with the title, as it did in the case of the scribes. Jesus' authority was based on what he was, rather than on what he appeared to be, on his inner disposition, not his external appearance. Likewise, the genuine authority of good preachers comes from who they are, rather than from the titles they hold, or the way they appear to society. In other words, authority comes from one's integrity, rather than academic degrees, listings in church bulletins, impressive business cards, or expensive clerical vestments. Korean preachers can exercise their authority only when the congregation trusts them as leaders and spokespersons regarding the spiritual and moral concerns of the community. Because the authority of preachers is intrinsically connected with the community they serve, let me begin with the authority of preachers in the Korean community.

The Authority of a Preacher in a Hierarchical Society

Like the Hebraic and early European societies, Korean society is still best characterized as a patriarchal hierarchy.

In spite of rapid Westernization, Korean society retains an ancient structural hierarchy. One of the reasons that the patriarchal and hierarchical structure persists is the Confucian orientation of Korean people. Confucianism came to Korea long before it became the "official" religion of the Korean people during the Yi Dynasty more than five hundred years ago. Confucianism is more than a religion, for it controls and legitimates the very fabric of personal, social, and political behaviors. Confucianism has been a way of life for the Korean people. The Confucian mode of thinking is so deeply implanted in the unconscious mind of the Korean people that it is difficult to change the Confucian mind-set, in spite of modernization.

A survey conducted among four hundred Korean Christians who live in the New York City area indicates that the Confucian system and values still persist among Korean Americans.[1] Although they live in America, their value system and lifestyle have not changed. This may have to do with the Confucian mind-set. As Hee-Sung Keel says, "No matter what religious affiliation one may have, all Koreans are practically Confucianists in the sense that they all follow Confucian norms of behavior and share Confucian moral values in their way of life and thinking."[2] From my experience in ministering to a Korean congregation, I discovered that Koreans in America consider egalitarianism a norm only when they work with American people. However, their behavior changes and they take on hierarchy as the norm when they gather as a group, such as a Korean congregation. Their unconscious mind-set of following Confucianism functions spontaneously when they are among other Koreans. Thus, the Korean Christian congregation in America is very much Confucian and retains patriarchal and hierarchical patterns of behavior and thinking.

Confucian values are based on a hierarchy. The five relationships that summarize human behaviors are all based on hierarchical order: the relationships between father and son, between husband and wife, between elder brother or sister and younger brother or sister, between older and younger persons, and between the ruler and the ruled. The hierarchical relationship is based on three basic determinants: sex, age, and rank. The dominance of the male over the female is manifested in the relationship between husband and wife, the dominance of the old over the young is manifested in the relationship between the elder and younger persons, and the dominance of the higher rank over the lower is demonstrated in the relationship between the ruler and the ruled. Among the five relationships, three relationships deal with family life. Among them the relationship between father and son is pivotal to all other relationships. When this relationship, which is sustained by filial piety, does not endure, the family cannot sustain itself. And it is said that when the family fails, the nation cannot stand, for the family is the foundation of society.[3] The authority of a preacher comes from the very structure of Korean society. If the father is the most powerful person in the family, and the family is the foundation of society, to be a father figure in the Korean community means to be the most powerful person in that community. The Korean preacher is often regarded as the father figure, the one who is the "head of the family." According to one woman cited by a Korean congregational study, the minister should be a father figure. She said, "In every family there should be a head of the family. And the head of the family has to be respected whether he is right or wrong."[4] The unconditional obedience to the head of the family is a typical attitude of Confucian mentality. Thus, the preacher, symbolically the head of the religious community, has unlimited power. As Jung Ha Kim says, "In terms of 'running' the religious organization, the minister's power is almost unlimited in the context of the Korean-American church, usually depending only on his [sic] intentions and willingness to maneuver various situations."[5]

Confucian hierarchical values also play an important role in deciding the authority of a preacher. A sexual determinant decides very much the authority of a preacher. Just as it is believed inappropriate for the female to be the head of the family, so too are women discouraged from being preachers in Korean congregations. Very few Korean congregations welcome women as their preachers. Moreover, age has a lot to do with a preacher's authority. It is generally understood that the older the preacher is, the more he or she is respected. In fact, many older people in the congregation do not want to have a young person as their preacher. Another determining factor in the hierarchy of authority is one's rank in the ecclesiastic world. Most Korean people take academic degrees very seriously. A prestigious congregation always prefers a preacher who has a doctoral degree. That is one of the reasons why there are so many Korean preachers who are working toward a doctoral degree in ministry. When a large and prestigious congregation, First Korean Church in Chicago, was looking for a new preacher, they considered only male candidates who were more than fifty years old, and who had completed a doctoral degree. Thus, Confucianism still lives in the Korean congregation in the United States. But the question is, How long will it persist in American society?

In hierarchical and patriarchal Korean society, authority is given by virtue of being a preacher. In this type of situation, the challenge is how not to become authoritarian. Genuine authority is realized when the preacher is accountable to the title that he or she holds, and is able to meet the expectations of the congregation. Also, the real authority of preaching should be vested not in the title, but in the ability that can be demonstrated to the congregation. The Korean congregation in America must eventually change from an authoritarian and hierarchical system to a more egalitarian and democratic structure as Koreans become more Americanized. As the church changes, second-generation Korean Americans will occupy an important place in congregational life. In order to meet this changing need, the preacher must be prepared to alter the patriarchal and hierarchical leadership style of today to the more egalitarian style of tomorrow.

The Servant of God and the Servant of People

I consider a preacher both the servant of God and the servant of people (although some preachers may disagree with me). During a retreat one summer, many Korean preachers who had been deeply influenced by the Confucian idea of a hierarchical value system, indicated that they thought of themselves as the heads of their congregations. They said that they would feel disgraced to have to think of themselves as the servants of people. "We must make clear," said one minister, "we are not servants of people. We are the servants of God!" As Korean preachers, we are products of hierarchical society, and it is natural for us to think that God's servants should also be the heads of our faith communities. However, it is a mistake to deny that we are also the servants of people. Most Korean preachers have in fact served our people, in addition to doing their sacred duties of preaching, administering sacraments, and other ecclesiastical functions. Moreover, to serve God means to serve people, for we cannot serve God without serving our neighbors. That is why service to God and service to humanity go hand in hand. In other words, to be the servant of God means to be the servant of people. Our authority as preachers is not vested in the titles or positions that we hold. Although the typical definition of servants means to belong to the lower class of society, we must recognize that our authority comes from our service to others. By serving God and people, we acquire our authority and respect, and our preaching becomes genuine.

In fact, we as Korean ministers in the immigrant church are both the servants of God and the servants of people. We are servants of God, because we are conscious of the genuine call of God in our ministry, and we take that call very seriously. Most of us would not willingly have chosen the ministry and preaching as our vocation. However, because we come from the conservative and evangelical tradition, we are emotionally and spiritually committed to God's call to service to the world. Likewise, most Korean students in my theological seminary went through serious spiritual struggles before they decided to enter the preaching ministry. Their experiences were similar to mine:

> I wrote letters to my father in Korea and told him of my decision to enroll in a theological seminary in order to become a Christian minister. My father wrote me again and again that I should continue my studies in chemistry. . . . I had to obey my father, but at the same time I had to obey the call of God to the ministry, too. Torn between the two conflicting demands, I did not know what to do. I struggled for several days and nights, praying and searching my heart for a solution. At the end I decided to give my loyalty to God and to his call to the ministry.[6]

What makes preachers different from other people is not so much the call of God itself but their commitment to that call. The call can be heard by others, but it is not realized until it is accepted and pursued. From an ecclesiastic perspective, a preacher's authority is bestowed at ordination. Although all believers of Christ can be called the servants of God, we as preachers are set apart or become explicit examples after being ordained to perform specific tasks assigned by the church. In this respect, the actual authority of preachers is given by the church or the congregation. Thus, preachers are also the servants of the congregation, because God in the form of Christ came first to serve. To be the servants of God, therefore, means to be the servants of people. It cannot be an either-or, but must be a both-and. To deny one is to deny the other. Thus, the servants of God and the servants of people are inseparable.

By serving people in all walks of life, our preaching becomes powerful and alive. Preaching does not deal with the naked word of God but with the embodied word, which embraces not only the witness of Christ but also our sacrifice to those whom we serve. Thus, whatever we do as preachers to our own congregations, we are doing to God: "Just as you did it to one of the least of these who are members of my family, you did it to me" (Matt. 25:40). Most Korean preachers who have immigrant congregations appear to have fulfilled the mandate of God: giving food to the hungry, giving drink to the thirsty, welcoming the stranger, clothing the naked, taking care of the sick, and visiting prisoners (Matt. 25:35-39).

During the 1960s and 1970s, the rapid expansion of the Korean immigrant population in the United States resulted in enormous problems of helping them adjust to this strange land. There were almost no social service organizations in this country which could assist Korean immigrants. Many Korean churches were organized and immediately took on the responsibility of helping the new immigrants. In the initial stage of developing their new congregations, preachers were responsible for almost everything: church organization, preaching and worship services, as well as social work, and the issues facing the new immigrants. Preachers became taxi drivers for the congregation, taking new immigrants where they needed to go, picking them up from airports upon their arrival from Korea, or buying their groceries, and so on. Preachers were interpreters, for most immigrants spoke no English. I spent many hours at the courthouse speaking on behalf of my church members who could not speak English. We also served as employment counselors. Since I was their minister, people asked me to help find them jobs. They wanted to work, and needed jobs for their survival. They didn't care what type of job it was.

Many Korean immigrants today are much more particular. And many Koreans continue to think of the preacher as a job finder or employment agent.[7] Korean preachers also acted as counselors and detectives. In one of my first congregations, the Korean wives of U.S. servicemen at the nearby Air Base had more domestic problems than most. They would call me even after midnight to settle their domestic conflicts and violence disputes. I had to call the police many times when I was unable to deal with the crisis by myself. On one occasion, I was asked to serve as a private detective for one of the women in my congregation.

My wife also took church members to grocery stores and showed them how to prepare food in their new homes. My experiences as a preacher of a small Korean congregation were not out of the ordinary. The things I did are fairly typical examples of the responsibilities and services that most Korean preachers were asked to perform during the 1960s and 1970s. Many Korean preachers in the Chicago area seemed to endure more troubles and hardships than I did. Some of us had to do these things in order to build and maintain our congregations. But many of us served our congregants out of compassion and concern for them as new immigrants in the United States.

I have learned that serving people is more than simply fulfilling the mandate of God to serve our neighbors. Through my experiences, I became closer to the members of my congregation, and learned to empathize with them and how to fight with them against injustice. Through the experience of serving them in various ways, I became a better preacher. I could reflect through preaching on the agonies, struggles, and pain that they suffered. Also, I could speak on an emotional and intellectual level that they could understand. My preaching became truly contextual, reflecting not only their experience but also the conditions under which they lived which were distinctively different from those of other people.

Most Korean preachers no longer serve their congregations as we did in the early 1970s. Because the Korean church is now well organized, most problems are handled by lay leaders, relatives, or friends in this country, and by social service organizations which have been established to serve new immigrants. Most Korean ministers can now concentrate their efforts in their offices rather than in the homes of their congregants. They have become more like professionals, posting office hours for counseling and for discussing church activities. In many cases, they are no longer closely in touch with the real-life situations, the struggles, and the pain of their congregants. I am saddened by what is currently happening in Korean ministry. Professionalism will eventually curtail the minister's authority in the Korean community, and the Korean church will become more like other churches in America. Certainly, no one can be all things to all people, and some specialization is inevitable in today's ministry. It is not a matter of how well or how professionally we serve, but how willing we are to serve. When the work of preachers is confined within the office or the church building, their preaching becomes insensitive, like water in a bucket. Water is alive when it flows, but becomes stagnant when it stops flowing. Just as the water contained in the bucket is contaminated, preaching that does not touch the real lives of people is inert, even though it may contain many good ideas. Unless we as preachers commit ourselves realistically to serving people, we cannot be true servants of God.

The Person of Spirit, a Shamanic Figure

Preachers are regarded as spiritual leaders whose power and authority come from the Spirit. The image of preachers as spiritual leaders is very strong in the Korean church, and is stressed much more among Korean preachers than among American ministers. Although it is difficult to understand where this idea came from, I suspect that it comes from two primary sources: from the evangelical and pietistic movement of the early American missionaries, and from the shamanic orientation of the Korean people. Somehow, the evangelical and pietistic fervor and Korean shamanic tradition seem to work together in many ways. They are, first of all, focused on the personal rather than the social dimension of religious growth. Both emphasize individualistic development of the religious consciousness. Second, both are emotive and emphasize feelings over reason. The Korean congregation loves revival meetings, all-night vigils, and prayer retreats, where emotion plays a leading role in the religious experience. Shamanism, like evangelical pietism, emphasizes emotion. Its primary aim is to bring the believer into an ecstatic state, where he or she experiences emotional liberation. Both evangelical pietism and shamanism use singing, bodily gestures, and prayers, as well as other means to intensify the emotional and spiritual experience. Although the similarities end when examining theological orientations, ethical issues, worldviews, and outlooks on life, both evangelical pietism and Korean shamanism have so much in common that many Korean ministers have no problem incorporating shamanism into their Christian faith.

Although the exclusive attitude of the early Christian movement in Korea rejected shamanism as Christianity's worst enemy, Christianity itself has many shamanistic characteristics. Shamanism was so pervasive in Jesus' time that his ministry can be viewed from a shamanic worldview. His miracles, his healing ministry, his power of exorcism, his vision search and temptation, and so on, are common elements of the work of any great shaman.[8] Although Jesus was more than a shaman, some things he did in his teaching reveal a shamanic character. In this respect, it is natural for preachers to have some characteristics of shamans, even though they must be more than shamans.

Because of the shamanic background of the Korean people, the congregation unconsciously expects a preacher to be a shamanic figure, even though they consciously reject shamanism. Thus, the preacher who becomes like a shaman or even pretends to be a shaman usually succeeds in bringing large crowds of people and large amounts of funds to the church. The preachers of many rapidly growing Korean churches in America are often suspected of being Christianized shamans, who use shamanic practices in Christian guise. Some of the so-called great preachers were shamanic figures. Elder Park, who preached to vast numbers of people in tent meetings, was a shamanized preacher. I recall attending one of his meetings, where thousands of people expected to receive blessings through visions and ecstatic experiences of meeting Christ. The content of his preaching came from the Christian Bible, but the interpretation of his message and the style of his preaching were shamanistic. Eventually, he established a sect known as the Oliver-Tree Movement. Sun-myong Moon is also a great shamanic preacher and is deeply interested in the movement of the Spirit. Eventually, he established the Unification Church. Many preachers of rapidly growing Korean churches today are shamans in Christian guise. Like shamans, they promise personal blessings through emotional and spiritual experiences in the church. As noted earlier, Paul Yonggi Cho, who claims to have the largest congregation in the world, is often known as a latter-day shaman who promises healing, wealth, and success in life.[9]

Shamanic preachers are authoritarian, stressing their personal power rather than yielding to the power of God. Shamans, relying on their tutorial god, have the power to summon the spirit or spirits and to demand their obedience. Shamans can travel from this world to the spiritual world and communicate with the spirits. They are persons of the spirit. Likewise, shamanic preachers rely on the Spirit to exercise their power and authority in the church. Peter Wagner's statement is partly applicable to shamanic preachers: "The pastor of a growing church is typically a strong authority figure, and that authority has been earned through living relationships with the people."[10] Shamanic preachers acquire their authority from the spirit through ecstasy, not through living relationships with the people. However, through that authority, the living relationship is established between shamanic preachers and their congregations. Many people will come to the church if the preacher is perceived to be as powerful as a shaman. For the Korean mind, the more powerful the shaman is, the more blessings the shaman can bring. That is why many growing churches are centered on powerful and authoritarian shamanic figures, who demand absolute obedience from their congregations. The following excerpt from a sermon illustrates the typical shamanic preacher in Christian guise:

> I will share a golden rule of all growing, successful churches on the face of this earth. It is the three-fold rule: one, obey your minister. Two, provide everything that he [sic] needs. Three, never go against him. If the church follows this three-fold rule, then you will experience a rapid growth of membership and God's unexpected blessings upon the church. . . . The relationship between lay members and God requires the mediator, the church minister . . .[11]

Just as the power and authority of shamans come from their tutorial god or tutorial spirit, shamanic preachers appeal for their authority to the Spirit or spirit. What gives them the authority to preach and to perform other religious functions is none other than the spirit. Ordination and ecclesiastic power are all relative to the power of the spirit. Retaining a harmonious congregation is not easy within the shamanic paradigm of leadership. Unless preachers are really powerful, congregations can easily split into different groups. Shamanic preachers must be as powerful as shamans, performing miracles, healing diseases, speaking in tongues, and doing many other things to persuade people that they are truly persons of the spirit. Shamanic preachers must be in control of spiritual matters over their people, and no one in their congregation should be able to contest their authority. As soon as someone challenges the preacher's spiritual power, there arises a great crisis in the church.

Let me illustrate this point using my own experience of ministry in a Korean congregation. I was never a shamanic preacher, even though most of my congregation wanted me to be shamanic in my style of preaching and administration. At the Air Base near the church, we had organized a Bible study group. Since it caused much inconvenience for me to pass through the gate of the Air Base as an outsider, I decided to allow one of the women to lead the group. I later discovered that she was a shamanic Christian who appealed to the spirit for her understanding of scriptures. Whenever she confronted a passage that she could not understand, she went into a room alone, closed the door, and prayed to the spirit. After the prayer, she came out and said to the group, "I talked to God and received the answer." Since they were shamanic in orientation, they believed her ability to speak to the spirit. She then developed the habit of talking with the spirit in prayers. When they talked about problems within the congregation, she said, "I will talk to God and find out." After prayer, she gave them an answer. Soon rumors began to spread around the Air Base and even to our congregation. Some of my congregation thought that she should tell me what to preach and what to do for the church, because she was more spiritual than I, and could directly speak to God. Her challenge was one of the most difficult ones I have had to deal with in my preaching ministry. Ultimately, the congregation realized that she was more disruptive than helpful for their spiritual development. As a result, she finally left the church. However, it took a long time to settle the issue, and was a most painful experience for all of us.

Spiritual Materialism: A New-Age Shaman

When the preacher is a shamanic figure, the congregation is centered on him or her. Shamanism is not an institutionalized religion. It is based on the clientele, who come to the shaman for the service. The greater the shaman is, the more people are willing to go to him or her. In the same manner, the greater a shamanic preacher is, the more people are willing to follow him or her. Thus, church growth is almost entirely dependent on the preacher. Moreover, the congregation belongs to the preacher, just as the shaman's clients belong to the shaman. Thus, most Korean people usually know the church by the name of its preacher rather than by the name of the church.

In fact, most Korean Americans make no clear distinctions between the minister and the church when they talk about what church means in their lives. For instance, it is not unusual at all for Korean Americans to claim that they belong to minister So-and-so's church, as if the church is a personal possession of the minister.[12]

Many shamanic preachers think that the congregation is their clientele, and the church building is their property. Like shamans, they operate the church as a business. The larger the clientele they have, the more income they bring in.

When I first arrived on the East Coast, I was told by a friend who had worked for a denominational church organization that most Korean churches in the area operated more like businesses. I soon discovered this to be true. Perhaps the Korean people who lived in the same area where I lived were more shamanistically oriented than those I meet in the Midwest. Those preachers were more like shamanic figures who have incorporated the sophisticated mentality of capitalistic and materialistic Western culture. Because shamanistic mentality and capitalistic materialism are brought together in their preaching ministry, their churches grow fast and become powerful. Whenever a shamanic preacher sees visitors, who are potentially new members, coming to his or her church, the first thing he or she thinks of is how much they can give to the church. In other words, the newcomers are often judged in terms of their wealth. This reminds me of a past visit to a well-known shaman in Korea. The first thing she asked me was how much money I could give for a *kut*, a shamanic ceremony. She asked me whether I would be willing to give a few thousand dollars. I said that I was not rich enough to pay that much, but I would pay a few hundred dollars for a *kut* for myself. She said, "I don't want to be bothered with a small *kut* like that." Shamanic preachers in this country would say the same thing, but they are sophisticated enough to express it elusively.

Let me relate another experience. When my wife and I first visited the church of a local shamanic minister, we were driving an old Dodge automobile. Because it was more than ten years old, the paint had faded. After the service, the minister came outside to send us off. As soon as he saw our car, he turned around and hurried back to the church without even saying good-bye. We were quite upset, because we had expected that he would at least ask us to come back. My wife said, "Why did he treat us like this? We are not worth a penny to him." More than a year later, we decided to visit the same church again. This time, we were driving a new car. The preacher did not recognize us. As is customary after the service, the preacher came out to send us off. When he saw our new car, he was kind enough to ask us to stay for coffee. We were in a hurry and decided not to stay. However, a few days later the preacher phoned and invited us to a church party. We did not attend. Certainly that preacher was a shamanic figure, looking for clients to expand his business. Just as the shaman uses the spirit to benefit his or her wealth, many preachers use the name of Christ to benefit their church business.

Moreover, the church can also be for sale. About twenty years ago one minister confided to me that he had paid ten thousand dollars to buy a church in America. "This was the only way," he said, "to come to America." In the early 1970s, when large numbers of immigrants began arriving from Korea, it was common practice to "buy" an established congregation. The minister who sells the church moves elsewhere to organize another church for sale. Like real estate developers, preachers with shamanic charm set up new congregations and then sell them to ministers looking for churches in this country. The primary job of the church developers was to organize new churches to later sell. When one congregation was sold, they simply set up another.

In recent years there has unfolded a new form of purchasing congregations without exchanging money. It is in the form of a bequest. When shamanic preachers move away or are promoted to better positions in the church, they pass their congregations on to their sons, brothers, brothers-in-law, or other relatives. Since shamanic preachers are so powerful, they can designate their successors, usually members of their family or one of their friends. Many congregations, in this respect, are the "property" of shamanic preachers who have learned the business of capitalistic materialism in America.

When preachers are discharged from the church by powerful lay elders and deacons, they sometimes move right next door to the church and start a new congregation, taking their loyal clientele with them. Faithful members follow their minister wherever he or she goes. Thus, when a preacher is fired, a new congregation is born. In this way the number of Korean congregations can multiply rapidly, while the actual number of Christians does not change. The same Christians move from one congregation to another when a congregation splits. Moreover, some rapidly growing churches raid small churches for members. Thus, small churches sometimes hesitate to release copies of their membership rosters to non-members, fearing that their congregants might be solicited by aggressive shamanic churches. Shamanic preachers always want more members, and thus more money, to secure their power and authority in the church. Because they think of the church as a business, the expansion of the church is also the expansion of their business.

The idea of the church as the preacher's possession begins as early as the inception of a congregation. It is the preacher who brings in his or her own clientele through home Bible studies or prayer meetings. The preacher is responsible for setting up the congregation, and the members of the congregation are obliged to stay with him or her. In other words, the preacher is not called by the congregation to serve. Rather, the congregation is called by the preacher. In this respect, the clergy placement systems used by a few of the large denominations are not always effective for Korean congregations.

Thus, the fundamental difference between shamanism and Christianity is ethics. Shamanism is a self-centered religion, while Christianity is a self-sacrificing religion. Shamanism can be thought of as a religion of "cheap grace." When Christianity is shamanized, it loses its soul. A shamanized Christianity is like a wolf in sheep's clothing. It is the most dangerous form of religion, because it eventually destroys Christianity itself. No matter how fast the congregation grows, or how much money the church makes, if that congregation is led by a shamanic preacher, it is far better to be a small congregation comprising a faithful few trying to survive in a world where large churches rule. It is fortunate that there are also many dedicated Korean preachers who honestly seek to restore the integrity of the Korean church and to provide leadership that will awaken the spiritual and moral conscience of the Korean people. These men and women are the hope for the future, the seeds of a new generation of Korean Christianity.

The Person of the Bible

The authority of a preacher comes from the Bible, the only book that Korean congregations believe truly reveals the will of God. This fundamentalistic view of the Bible is so deeply ingrained in the minds of Korean Christians that whatever is said in the pulpit must be supportable by scripture. The preacher, therefore, uses biblical quotations to prove the point. The more he or she uses biblical quotations in preaching, the more powerful the preaching is perceived to be. The preacher is expected to read, study, and understand the Bible better than the members of the congregation. The qualification of a preacher is primarily his or her knowledge of the Bible. For most laypeople, a theological education means learning the Bible. The more degrees in theology the preacher has, the more he or she should know about the Bible.

Because the preacher is a person of the Bible, he or she can never leave the Bible at home. Wherever the preacher goes, he or she must take the Bible along, because the preacher is expected to read from the Bible in many unexpected places. The preacher is asked to read the Bible during home visitations, casual parties, at sickbeds in the hospital, at the birth of children, while counseling troubled couples, at public gatherings, at various church-related services, and so forth. In almost all cases, the preacher is expected to read the Bible, because people believe that the Bible becomes more meaningful when it is read by the preacher. The preacher not only needs to carry the Bible all the time, but he or she also needs to know the Bible well enough to pick passages relevant to particular occasions. Occasionally, a layperson will test whether the preacher knows the Bible better than he or she does, by asking, "Where can we find the passage of so-and-so in the Bible?" If the preacher fails to answer the question, the interrogator thinks he or she is not competent. That is why most Korean preachers seem to know the Bible from cover to cover. They memorize important passages and recognize immediately where to find them. It is, therefore, an important requirement for a preacher to read the Bible ceaselessly and to memorize as many passages as possible. Although the preacher may not find time to read the newspaper, he or she ought to read the Bible every day, not merely to nurture his or her spiritual life, but to stay ahead of the laity.

However, the authority of a preacher as a person of the Bible comes not only from knowing the facts and memorizing important verses of the Bible; his or her real authority comes when the preacher becomes the interpreter of the Bible in a given context. When laypeople find a scriptural passage irrelevant in their thinking, or two contradicting statements in the Bible, they almost always ask the preacher to provide answers. In this kind of situation, a theological education becomes very important. One evening an older woman, who was the mother of several adult children, came to a Bible study group and, while pointing to Mark 3:31-35, asked about Jesus' attitude toward his mother. "How could he simply dismiss his mother when she came to look for him? How can you respect one who does not respect his own mother?" From the perspective of Korean culture, which values the family above all other units of life, Jesus' dismissal of his own mother for the sake of affirming the universal family made no sense to her at all. If the preacher teaches the Bible with true authority (unlike someone who simply memorizes the verses), he or she must help people like this older woman find a deeper meaning of the passage which will satisfy her question. Thus, the Korean preacher begins to realize that the authority of preaching and teaching comes not only from knowing the text, but also from finding a meaningful interpretation of the text in the context of our time.

Preacher as a Prophet and Leader of Community

If all Korean preachers were shamanic figures, there would be no hope in the Korean church. However, there are also prophetic figures who combat the corruption of the church and speak for justice and the liberation of the poor and oppressed. One of the prophetic movements dissenting against the self-centered and status quo–seeking church is a movement called minjung theology. Minjung theology was born in the 1970s out of the human rights struggles in South Korea. *Minjung* means "a mass of people," or more specifically, the people who are controlled and oppressed by the powerful or the elite.[13] Like the prophetic voices in the Old Testament, and reminiscent of Latin American liberation theology, minjung theologians stress political, economic, and social action to change oppressive social structures. Although they are in the minority, their voices are heard and taken seriously.

The same kind of prophetic activities are taking place in the Korean church community in America. Since more than 70 percent of the Korean population in America attends church, the church is where action must occur. Because preachers are the "heads of the church," they are the most powerful members of community life. The leadership of preachers directly affects not only the lives of Korean peoples, but also their image in America. Great community leadership must come from preachers, as has been the case in the African American church. The emergence of preachers as Korean community leaders is beginning to take place all over the United States. In almost all cases, preachers either initiate or become leaders in the formation of national and community organizations. There are almost no Korean community organizations in which preachers are not involved.

In New York City, for example, there are a significant number of Korean preachers who have long been deeply involved in the liberation of Korean Americans from their status as a weak, poor, and powerless ethnic minority. These preachers move beyond the walls of the church building and seek to create justice in their community and beyond. They have led demonstrations opposing injustices committed against Korean grocers and fruit sellers. They have helped arrange meetings between the Korean community and black leaders to attempt to reconcile ethnic conflicts. They have organized support groups for political and social action, and protested injustice with respect to racial and immigrant issues.

When I was the preacher of a Korean congregation, I also served as a member of the Board of Directors for the Multi-Ethnic Support Association and Community Housing Resources Board, which was appointed by the U.S. Department of Housing and Urban Development to support and enforce the fair housing policy in our community. There, I first learned how serious the problem of racial discrimination was in housing and in other areas of American life. Because of my involvement in community affairs, I could help my congregation become conscious of racism through my preaching and my actions. I organized demonstrations by members of my congregation whenever we recognized injustice toward ethnic minorities in our community. Once I took a retired Air Force serviceman to court because of his mistreatment of his Korean wife, who had been ruthlessly beaten by him and his mother simply because she was Korean and did not understand the American way of life. Several lay members of our congregation accompanied me to court to demonstrate our solidarity. Because we cared for one another as Christians and as ethnic minorities in this country, our church was alive and became an important center of social action.

Prophetic ministry does not end with preaching in the pulpit. Preaching must be taken into the field, where the action is. It must be more than a delivery of Good News to the poor. It is more than merely communicating the gospel or expounding the scripture. Prophetic ministry must challenge social injustice, engage in the actual continuing struggle for liberation, and share the pain and anger of those who are victims of unjust social structures. Korean preaching is meant to be prophetic and to break open the incarceration of the congregation to shamanic interests. As Korean preachers we must expand our horizons beyond the four walls; the community must be our congregation. This is the vision that the Korean church must uphold and move toward in the future as we approach the twenty-first century.

As I close this chapter, I realize that our genuine authority as preachers is not given to or bestowed on us at ordination. Our real authority as preachers is simply who we are as servants of God and of our congregations, and comes from the trust of the people whom we serve. The authority of Korean preachers that is built on the patriarchal and hierarchical structure of Confucian teachings will undoubtedly collapse as Koreans become more Americanized. Korean preachers must relinquish authoritarian leadership and learn to be more egalitarian. Moreover, it is crucial that we train and develop lay leadership. Instead of placing Christ at the center of the church, many shamanic preachers discourage lay participation and put themselves at the center. Their self-interest in the guise of spiritual and emotional charm misguides the congregation and snatches away the souls of innocent people. What is needed is for Korean preachers to combine the spiritual and emotional exhilaration of shamanic skills, with the Christian ethic of self-giving service. Moreover, we should not base our authority on the Bible. Rather, we should teach the Bible with authority. As Korean preachers we should not become like the scribes who received their authority from scripture, using it to maintain the status quo. We must bring scripture alive as the living Word incarnate in the real lives of those who are struggling for justice and peace in this world.

CHAPTER 6

KOREAN PREACHING IN TRANSITION

It is a common inclination among older adults to resist change, because change brings risk and uncertainty. On the other hand, for many young people change means challenge and new possibilities in their lives. Those who support Korean-speaking congregations are primarily older people who are recent immigrants to America. More than half the members in Korean congregations are people who came to America within the last ten years; and more than 95 percent of Korean Americans are first-generation immigrants.[1] They speak Korean, eat Korean food, see Korean movies, and listen to Korean music, and they want to maintain their normal day-to-day lives in America.

Because the socialization of most Korean people takes place within the church, the Korean church is not only the custodian of Korean culture but also an institution which preserves the traditional life of the Korean people. Therefore, change in the church means change in the congregation's lifestyles as well. As a result, people often do everything they can to resist change, although they know it is impossible to halt change entirely. The church as a social institution must change because society is constantly changing. Also, the immigrants themselves are changing, even though they do not see the changes taking place within themselves. Psychologically, they want to remain the same. This psychological factor is typically so powerful that the church seems to be the last fortress in America where they can defend their illusory safety. Because of the need to reassure and create a haven for older-generation Koreans, the church in America seems to be changing at a slower pace than the church in Korea, when in reality the former changes faster than the latter.

In order to forestall changes, many Korean preachers in America bring ultraconservative fundamentalist preachers from Korea to lead revival meetings, to participate in pulpit exchanges, and to speak at various church and church-related affairs. These preachers from Korea are well respected and honored, because they seem to bear the authority of authentic Korean preaching. More people attend church services when a guest preacher is invited from Korea, because he or she can speak more "authentic" Korean and inform the congregation about what is happening in Korea. Many Korean preachers in America want to secure their position of power by reinforcing patriarchal and hierarchical values, which are not only embodied by the very presence of the speaker from Korea but also supported by his preaching.

However, any attempt to halt change can only be temporary. The church must change and is in fact changing, because even those wanting to stop change are themselves changing in spite of their resistance. Nothing can stop the change process, since change is the very principle that keeps us alive. Thus, the unchanging congregation will die. Like a plant with its roots cramped in too small a pot, it can neither live long nor grow tall. Many Korean congregations in America are like such plants. They must be transplanted into American soil if they really want to thrive. None of us wants to leave the soil in which we grew up, but it is imperative that we be transplanted in new soil. It takes courage to face new challenges, as well as pain and struggle. A willingness to be transplanted is the only way Korean immigrants can survive in this country and cultivate their future possibilities. Therefore, we, as responsible preachers, must encourage congregations to change, knowing that it takes courage and grace to make a drastic change, which implies the transplantation of the Korean lifestyle into American life. This means that we should not preach the type of sermons that we have preached before, for the context has changed and is changing. Thus, Korean preaching must be transformed if it is to be truly alive and nurture the changing needs of Korean people in America.

Preaching Toward the Americanization of the Korean People

Realizing that the church can survive only when it changes, it is our responsibility as Korean preachers to challenge the congregation to change rather than to reinforce a patriarchal and hierarchical value system which does not work in this country. Certainly, change here does not mean indiscriminately adopting American values. It means creatively adopting new values, and adapting them to meet the greater possibilities of new life in America.

In order to transform our congregations, we must first change ourselves, so that our preaching also changes. Without changing ourselves, our preaching does not change, for preaching is the disclosure of our embodied self before the congregation. The Americanization of our lifestyle demands more than simply transforming our psychological and emotional attitude. We must equip ourselves to be aware of American values and participate in the actual life of American people. In order to do this, Korean preachers should regularly attend continuing education programs which emphasize multicultural issues and the Americanization of immigrants. We must not perpetuate ministerial continuing education programs in the Korean church which attempt to halt change, such as conservative Bible study, evangelism, church growth, and so on. Although some of these programs are important for our preparation for preaching, we must focus on more contextual studies in our continuing education programs, in order to facilitate the transition of our congregations from Korean to Korean American.

We must learn to write and read English as proficiently as possible. One of the many requirements for us as Korean preachers is to read English newspapers as well as Korean papers daily. Most of us do not read English newspapers because it takes time and patience for us to read in English. Moreover, many of us do not feel any urgency about reading or writing in English, because we feel we can function as Korean ministers without using the English language in preaching and other ecclesiastical activities. However, we must force ourselves to read newspapers in English, and to attend lectures and other continuing education programs offered in English. We cannot enlarge our vision as ministers in transition if we limit ourselves to only reading Korean newspapers, or attending Korean continuing education programs, or listening to Korean news on the radio or television. Since we live in America and are leaders in the Korean American community, we must learn to speak, read, and write in English. Moreover, we must change our social habits. We must force ourselves to attend social gatherings where many different ethnic Americans come together, and to educate ourselves in an effort to become Korean Americans. Unless we, as preachers, change ourselves, our preaching will not be able to meet the challenge of our changing congregations. And if we cannot change, we must seriously consider retiring from the preaching ministry. This will allow younger Korean American preachers who have graduated from American theological seminaries to replace us, and facilitate the process of transition as efficiently as possible.

Korean preachers should also know the history of Asian and Korean immigration in America. Understanding the immigration history of the Korean people in this country is helpful for our transition from the present to the future. Since the history of Korean immigration is neither found in school textbooks nor taught in public school systems, it is especially our responsibility as Korean ministers to preach and teach the history of Korean immigration in this country to our people and to help them accept it as a part of our history.[2] Besides preaching and teaching about the difficulties of immigrant life for the newly arrived, we must also form special study groups to fully explore other aspects of immigrant life. We must learn how the early immigrants suffered, were rejected, humiliated, and stereotyped because they looked and acted differently. Through this knowledge we can better appreciate the opportunity of freedom we are experiencing, and also view ourselves more realistically in this country. We, as Korean preachers, must help our people make an effort to transform the stereotype of Koreanness into a wholesome image of true humanity. As Korean immigrants, we are bound both to Korea and to America, because we are Korean in ethnicity and American in nationality. Thus, the history and culture of Korea alone constitutes only half of our life. The other half of our life belongs to American history and culture. Our roots are in Korea, but our branches are in America. That is why we must preach not only what it means to be a Korean, but also what it means to be an American. Because we are transplanted into the American landscape, the Korean church must grow from American soil. It is our responsibility as ministers of the gospel to transform others by transforming ourselves and by creating a new image and environment which will improve our lives in this country.

Our preaching must reflect this new change. We cannot continue to preach a message that treats our people as if they are still living in Korea. We as ministers must remind our people again and again that we are not sojourners, but permanent dwellers in this country. We will be buried in this land, and our children and grandchildren will be born in this country. Because we are transplanted into new soil, we must preach a new message from the pulpit, not the same old message that reminds us of Korea. The new message that first-generation Koreans must hear from the pulpit is the message of being pioneers in America. We must celebrate Thanksgiving Day as our holiday, because we are now American citizens. If we instead celebrate the fifteenth of August on the lunar calendar, the Korean Thanksgiving Day, then we should also celebrate the arrival of the first Korean immigrants in Hawaii more than a hundred years ago as our ethnic thanksgiving day. I once preached a Thanksgiving Day sermon, "Our Thanksgiving Day," in an effort to encourage my Korean listeners to be pioneers in this country:

> Pioneers are people who don't go back to their homeland when they face problems and troubles in the new land. Pioneers are those who have made up their mind to stay for good in the new land. They have the faith of Abraham. They are not conformists but cultivators of a new land. We have to cultivate the wilderness if we are pioneers. Our wilderness is a society of injustice and prejudice, like a desert that is hot in the day but cold in the night. Just as the California desert was transformed into a rich soil, where many fruit trees and vegetables grow, we can and must cultivate this society to be a truly loving and caring place to live.[3]

It is important to take sermon topics from immigrant themes in scripture. The life of the Hebrew people was filled with the theme of immigration. The immigration of Abraham and Sarah to the land of Canaan, the immigration of their descendants into Egypt, living in the wilderness for forty years, immigrating to the promised land, and so on, are important stories of Hebraic history. By using scripture texts which relate immigration experiences, we can offer parallels to the history of Korean immigration in the United States.

Preaching on Identity Crises

As long as Koreans in America do not take seriously that we are living in America as Korean Americans, then we are not conscious of the fact that we are having an identity crisis. Most of the immigrants who live in the Korean section of Los Angeles do not feel that they have an identity crisis, because they live in Los Angeles just as if they were living in Seoul, Korea. Thus, Korean Town in Los Angeles is often called Little Seoul, where people do not have to speak English, socialize with Americans of other ethnic groups, shop at American groceries, or eat at American restaurants. However, after they are made aware of the fact that their town is only a small part of the larger American society, a society which influences their lives, they can then start to forge their identity in the larger society. Korean Americans who view their life in America realistically do not deny the problem that an identity crisis exists.

One of my Korean theology students discovered the following on a wall hanging:

> Am I a Korean?
> No.
> Am I an American?
> No.
> Who am I?

After reading it, he decided to focus his ministry on helping those who seek their identity as Korean Americans. This crisis is real to those who take their lives in this country seriously. We know that our roots are in Korea because of our ethnic and racial origins. We also know that we are Americans because we are American citizens. Nevertheless, we are not fully accepted as Americans, because of our racial and ethnic origins. American people still ask me, "Where do you come from?" If I say that I come from Ohio, they are not satisfied with my answer. When I say, "I come from Korea," then they are satisfied. Although I have lived and worked in America for forty years, other Americans do not accept me as an American. This does not mean that I am completely Korean either. I have come to realize that I have changed and have become Americanized. Thus, I am neither totally Korean nor American. Who am I? Many years ago, after reflecting upon my experience as someone who belongs to neither America nor Korea, I told my congregation:

> English is not my mother tongue. People instantly notice that I am a foreigner when they hear my speech. . . . I cannot laugh the way Americans laugh. I cannot cry the way they do. I often miss the joke. I cannot catch all the humor of their remarks. . . . I have also a different way of thinking and a different value system because I come from a different culture. I love tranquillity more than excitement. I love nature more than man-created things. I like certain kinds of food and music that most Americans shun. Therefore, I live and work with Caucasians but I am not a part of their company. I am an alien. . . . Because of my intense nostalgia I have returned to my native country more than a few times. However, I have also found that the land where I grew up has changed substantially. The people with whom I grew up have changed. . . . I have become a stranger, an alien, in my land. . . . I have come to realize that I have no homeland at all. I am not really a Korean, because I am an American; I am not really an American, because I am a Korean in America. In fact, I am a Korean American, who is neither American nor Korean.[4]

By reflecting on my own experience, I wanted to make my congregation aware of the fact that they are also seekers of their own identity as Korean Americans, as neither Koreans nor Americans. We, Korean Americans, are hyphenated persons, we are in-between. We are between this world and that world, just as Jesus did not fully belong either to his homeland or to that of the Gentiles. Because Jesus was a marginal person, he helps us cope with our marginality.[5]

Jesus' message is that we can overcome our marginality through God's affirmation of our being, regardless of who we are. Our origin, our ethnicity, and the difference of our culture do not make us inferior. All of us are children of God, having received different gifts of ethnicity, which are the very designs of God's creation. Accepting who we are as God's gift, we can overcome our alienation from both our own homeland and our adopted country. It is, then, faith in God as the common father of all humanity that makes us truly accept our destiny beyond existential conditions. Korean preaching offers life and hope, and nurtures self-confidence and spiritual strength so that we may affirm our heritage as God's gift, and accept the challenge that this land is also God's gift for us. From this perspective, we are no longer "in-between" but "in-both." We, Korean Americans, are both Koreans and Americans at the same time.

Korean preaching must stress the virtues of a Korean American identity to counterbalance the negative aspects of being marginal. Our preaching should not end with the negative aspects of our identity, just as a sermon on the judgment of God must be followed by one on the hope of salvation. Likewise, our identity is defined as neither Korean nor American, but both Korean and American at the same time.[6] In other words, as preachers we must preach the affirmation of full humanity; we are fully Koreans and fully Americans simultaneously. This affirmation, which comes from a spiritual and faith-filled conviction, must be preached and acted out in the church. Being both Koreans and Americans, we can make contributions to the future of this country. We can bring our rich spiritual, religious, and cultural resources to America.

Our task is to cultivate American society and plant the seeds of Asian values for the creation of new humanity, by bringing about the creative synthesis of Asian culture and the soil of

122

Western society. . . . We brought many different seeds from
Korea, the seed of filial piety, the seed of respect for the old,
the seed of mystic insight, the seed of generosity, and the seed
of aesthetic intuition. We cannot guarantee that all these
seeds will grow. However, if we combine the best seeds from
Korea and the best soil available in America, we may be able
to produce one of the most beautiful gardens in the world.[7]

Preaching on the positive image of Korean American people can boost our collective self-esteem and give us the
courage to confront issues with confidence. Even the conversion experience that we, as Korean preachers, are interested
in can be understood in terms of the transforming experience
of a Korean American identity. Many texts in the Bible can
be interpreted creatively by presenting an affirmation of the
inclusion of Koreans in America.

If Korean Americans are new creations, they are more than
Koreans or Americans. Korean preachers must develop a
new style of preaching, which synthesizes both Korean and
American preaching styles. I do not know exactly what kind
of style this should be, but it must be a style that is distinctive
in itself, which meets the needs of a new generation of
Korean Americans and contributes to the fuller and richer
humanity of all people. As Korean preachers, we must also
transform ourselves to become new creations, those God has
intended us to be: people of integrity, human beings free of
captivity to injustice. The search for this new humanity as
Korean American preachers is a task that must be taken
seriously if the Korean church is to transform itself into the
church of the next generation.

Preaching More on Justice Issues and Praxis

It is more comfortable for Korean preachers to preach on
the spiritual and personal needs of people and to dismiss

social and political issues as irrelevant to religious concerns. A strong emphasis on shamanic preaching, which arouses people's emotions and comforts their psychological needs, is effective for the older generation, who continue to think as they did when living in Korea. However, our congregations, even those of the older generation, must confront many social, political, economic, and ethical issues as they work toward a fully participatory life in America. One of the most crucial issues that Korean Americans face, like most ethnic minorities in America, is the problem of racism. Class and gender issues are also directly related to many racial issues for Korean Americans. Racism makes Korean Americans marginal persons. It is our responsibility as preachers to speak out against racism, to proclaim it as one of society's worst evils. Racism is a most serious sin because it is a rejection of God's creative design. God created each of us to be different. To rank people's worth on the basis of racial origin is in fact to deny and reject God's creative design. This denial and rejection is fundamental to all other sins. That is why we must deal with racism from the perspective of creation. To avoid the topic of racism in preaching is none other than to avoid preaching on sin. I have never heard preaching in the Korean pulpit that did not speak of sin. In most cases when we preach about sin, we usually mean the moral sin of individuals. However, if we are truly concerned about sinfulness, we must be willing to preach about racism as sin against God's creation.

We, as Korean Americans, should not think that we ourselves are innocent of racism merely because we are also its victims. We also display racism toward other minorities in the United States. Whether we call it ethnocentrism or racism, white Americans are not the only racists. In other words, our preaching on racism should begin with repentance rather than judgment. As Christians, we must learn not to speak about racism with hate, but with love. In preaching on racism, we should learn to use a liberationist interpretation of scriptures, especially that of minjung theology,[8] which attempts to speak on behalf of the oppressed, the poor, and those who are the objects of discrimination. It is always helpful to illustrate sermons with personal experiences of discrimination, as well as with the structural discrimination that affects all ethnic minorities in this country. Korean ministers must take the time to study a variety of literature dealing with liberation movements and with racism in this country when preparing sermons on racism. It is also important to have cooperative services and gatherings with multiethnic groups in mutual support of human rights and racial justice for all. For preaching must be a part of praxis, which includes action. Preaching itself is an act of Christian love in its attempt to liberate people from every oppressive condition of humankind.

Because of its conservative evangelical orientation, the Korean church has in the past been interested in the universal implications of the biblical text for all persons, regardless of their social, cultural, or ethnic orientations. This kind of propositional and deductive approach in Korean preaching cannot be perpetuated in our multicultural society. As an ethnic minority group, we, the Korean American people, should understand that the same text can be understood differently by different people because of their different contexts. For example, encouraging servants to obey their masters or women to submit to men is offensive to both subjugated ethnic minorities and to contemporary women. Biblical texts can be used to oppress as well as to liberate. As a minority population in this country, we must find other ways to read the Bible, from our minority perspective, and to reinterpret it meaningfully for our present life situations. We must make a transition from a text-centered approach to a contextual understanding of the text in our preaching. This transition is an approach "from below" rather than "from above." This change is important for making our faith truly accountable to the context in which we exist in America. In this approach, preaching is none other than a biblical and theological reflection on the Christian witness and a praxis of living example. In other words, our life experience must be the basis of our preaching. Korean preaching in the twenty-first century must change its emphasis from the textual to the praxis approach, from the personal to the corporate approach, and from an emotive to a pragmatic approach to life.

Interpreting biblical texts on the basis of praxis means to divert the shamanistic mentality that seeks an inner satisfaction, and to turn toward an action-oriented life that emphasizes service to the world. The shamanic approach emphasizes ecstatic experience, as a means of resolving unresolved anger and resentment for innocent victims, for members of an ethnic minority struggling to live in an unjust and racist society.[9] A more realistic solution for this innocent suffering is not to escape into the temporary experience of ecstasy but to work to restore justice. The trance or ecstatic state is merely a temporary solution to the suffering created by injustice. True, lasting justice is not possible without action. That is why Korean preaching must focus more on our responsibility for transforming an unjust society into a just one. We must begin with the realignment of our energy from self-directed consumption based on our inner orientation, to service-directed production based on an outer orientation. Self-directed consumption means that all our energy is spent in satisfying our inner feelings. Through this self-direction we invest time and energy only on activities of the church itself. Thus the church and its members become the object of this self-service. On the other hand, service-directed production means that all our energy will be directed toward the work of serving and changing the world. The church needs both forms of commitment, but the emphasis should be on transforming the self-directed approach into a service-directed approach as the Korean church moves toward the twenty-first century.

At the present time, Korean preaching devotes itself to satisfying the emotional needs of people and sustaining the church itself. The so-called church growth idea has been based on a self-directed or self-serving approach, in which all energy is spent benefiting the church itself. Because it is self-serving, the emphasis on church growth for its own sake is destructive. Since the numerical growth of membership and financial giving are emphasized, the church feeds itself and becomes like an obese person who has difficulty moving around. In its insatiable obesity, the church requires more members to help it move, which then make it more obese. That is why many rapidly growing churches raid small churches for members. Just as the obese person demands more food, the rapidly growing church needs more members and activities. The more church activities that occur, the more sermons and meditations the preacher must prepare, so that all that preachers have time for is the internal work of the church. They have to preach at early morning prayer meetings every day, all night prayer meetings, midday worship services, Bible studies every Friday, Wednesday evening worship services, and Sunday morning and evening worship services. Likewise, the laypeople are so wrapped up in the various activities in the church that they have no time to rest. They are too tired to do anything outside the church community. The laity are deprived of precious hours to spend with their children. Although most Koreans came to this country to secure better education for their children, once they are caught up in the church, the children are often forgotten and end up growing up alone and without their parents at home because of their involvement in church activities. Many children, therefore, fail to attain a high standard of scholastic achievement. Some of them become juvenile delinquents, and some even run away from home. The church has created problems in the domestic and social lives of its members, because it consumes all of their energy.

Because many Korean preachers think that prayer meetings and worship services make the church grow, whenever church growth falters or attendance declines, they offer early morning prayer meetings, midday worship services, or Bible study groups. When I visited a church in Oakland, California, the preacher of that church told me, "I have to start more prayer meetings to increase attendance." I knew the church very well, because I had attended it regularly when the former pastor was there. I also knew that church attendance was declining primarily because of the conservative and fundamentalistic preaching of the present pastor. The more preachers establish prayer meetings and worship services, the more time they have to devote to the church and the more they absorb the energies and time of the laypeople. As the church grows and accumulates money, it erects new buildings and then increases its institutional programs to expand the church's power. The more buildings the church constructs and the more internal activities the church undertakes, the more it expands itself as an institution. In this way, the church feeds itself without ever actively engaging in the work of justice and peace in the world.

Just as an obese person needs exercise to become lean and healthy, the church also needs to divert its energy toward action in the world. The church will become spiritually and physically healthy when it becomes a servant to the world. Any self-serving church is not only self-destructive but also is destructive of the world. Korean preaching in the twenty-first century should focus on the world rather than on the church itself. The church must serve the world, rather than the world serving the church.[10] Korean preaching must, therefore, reflect on the praxis of justice and service for peace for humankind.

Preaching on Religious and Cultural Pluralism

During my visit to Chong-gyo Methodist Church in Seoul, Korea, in 1994, I had an opportunity to talk with the senior minister of that church, who was also a bishop in the Korean Methodist Church. He related that the Protestant church in Korea experiences difficulty because of religious pluralism. He said with great concern, "We have taught our people that Jesus Christ is the only way to God, and the God of Christianity is the only true God, since the inception of the Protestant church here over a hundred years ago. If we say to them now that other religions are also valid, they will believe we have been deceiving them. They will lose confidence in us, and in Christianity. There will be great chaos in the church. We do not know what to do. This is a critical moment in the history of Korean Christianity." This illustrates how the Korean Protestant church clings to the absolutistic and fundamentalistic approach to the Christian faith. Many Christians in Korea have already noticed that the Protestant church as a whole is too exclusive. They are unhappy with the church's stand on other religions, particularly those which are part of their own heritage. They are leaving the church and finding other, more inclusive religions to satisfy their spiritual needs. Thus, the membership of the Protestant church in Korea is declining. On the other hand, the Catholic church, which recognizes the validity of other religions, and Buddhism, which is open to other religions, are growing rapidly in South Korea.

In view of this development in Korea, the Korean church in America is more vulnerable than the Protestant church in Korea. The Korean church in America is, as I have already mentioned, even more fundamentalistic and exclusive than the church in Korea. Yet on the other hand, the American people as a whole are more tolerant of religious and cultural diversities, because they live in a multicultural society. In this age of pluralism, the Korean church in America has isolated itself and built a fortress around the church to prevent the exchange of multicultural influence. The question is, How long will the Korean church in America fortify itself against cultural and religious pluralism? If this kind of isolation continues, it will be disastrous to the church, and may eventually lead to the development of a cultic religion, the product of an ultra-exclusive religious community no longer in touch with the cultural mainstream of American life. Although religious fundamentalism itself has always been a part of American life, it is not in many cases isolated from American culture. In other words, American religious fundamentalism is quite different from Korean fundamentalism. The former is a part of American culture, while the latter is not. The Korean church in America is even more threatened by pluralism than is the church in Korea or the fundamentalistic church in America. The longer the Korean church in America delays, the harder it will be to deal with pluralism. The transition from an exclusive to an inclusive approach to other religions is crucial and needs special attention by all Korean preachers in this country.

How can we, as Korean preachers, facilitate this transition from a fundamentalistic and exclusive approach to an inclusive and open-ended approach to other religious traditions? Should we tell our congregations that what we have preached and taught about the absoluteness of Christ is wrong? Certainly not. The problem is not the absoluteness of Christ but exclusiveness. Christ is the truth, but exclusivism is only one way of knowing the truth. Thus, we need to change our way of thinking. The exclusive way of thinking defines truth by excluding others, but the inclusive way of thinking explains it by including them. Let me explain, using the simple example of the relationship between Christ and Buddha. In thinking exclusively, we define Christ as the truth by eliminating Buddha. Thinking inclusively, we can say Christ is truth because he includes Buddha. The exclusive way is an *either-or* approach, but the inclusive way is a *both-and* perspective. In fact, the either-or approach is incapable of knowing God, who is beyond the logic of either this or that. God is discernible to us through the both-and approach, because God is both transcendent and immanent.[11]

Either-or thinking is closely akin to the Western way of knowing the truth, while both-and thinking is an Asian way of approaching the truth. The both-and way of thinking is a holistic approach and very natural to Korean indigenous thinking, which is different from the traditional "either-or" thinking in the West. The Korean people have long used the both-and way of thinking symbolized in yin and yang, the symbol of Tae-guk, the emblem of the national flag.[12] It is, therefore, natural for the Korean people to change from an exclusive to an inclusive way of thinking about God. Korean preachers should help laypeople rediscover the Asian way of thinking through preaching and teaching, without sacrificing the ultimate commitment to Christ as the truth.

In introducing this new way of thinking (which is actually the recovery of old and indigenous thinking), we must be conscious and critical of the either-or way of thinking that fosters division and isolation in life. In order to explain the advantage of the both-and approach, we must provide many examples from our life experience to our laypeople. For example, as Korean Americans, we cannot be either Koreans or Americans, but we must be both Koreans and Americans at the same time. Certainly, the holistic and inclusive way of thinking must be reflected in our preaching and teaching. To supplement preaching and teaching, we must form discussion groups, as an alternative to the traditional Bible study groups, to introduce people to the inclusive "both-and" thinking for reflecting upon our Christian faith. Guest speakers should be invited, and various literature on inclusive approaches should be introduced to these groups. My hope is that these groups can become catalysts for transforming Korean congregations from an exclusive to an inclusive way of thinking about God, Christ, and various precepts of the Christian faith.

Another approach for introducing the inclusive way of thinking is through a serious study of Korean history and cultural tradition. To be Korean Christians means to be more than the people of the Bible, because we are not only Christians but also Koreans at the same time. Because we are both people of the Bible and people of Korea, we must study not only the Bible but Korean culture as well. In a multicultural society, what distinguishes us from others is our cultural roots. The Korean church, as the custodian of Korean culture in America, must be the place to learn the history and culture of Korea. Just as almost every Korean church provides a Korean language class for young people, the cultural tradition of Korea also must be taught and discussed in the church. By studying Korean culture, we rediscover our inclusive religious tradition. Shamanism, Buddhism, Taoism, and Confucianism are all a part of our tradition. We do not have to accept these religions anew, because they are already a part of our tradition. What we need is simply to acknowledge them as our own. In other words, other religions are not alien. We have simply ignored or rejected them, because we were thinking in terms of the exclusive either-or. A serious study of our own tradition helps us recover the coexistence of other religions in our lives. We should eventually accept Christianity as a Korean religion, just as other religions have become Korean religions. When we accept Christianity as a Korean religion or as a religion of the world, we can accept pluralism and coexist with other cultural groups in America. This does not mean that we give up our ultimate commitment to Christ, but our commitment will be open-ended rather than closed.

Some of the suggestions that I have made can be useful for the Korean church in making the transition from an exclusive approach to an open-ended approach to other religions. This issue is crucial for the survival of the Korean church in America, and preachers should not ignore its implications. A fundamentalistic and exclusive approach to Christianity may appear to help the church grow at the present moment, but this approach will eventually doom the church. Therefore, Korean Christians in America must wake up and see themselves as they really are. We are of many religions. We are, by our very nature, pluralistic and multicultural. This recognition of who we are is the beginning of our transition from isolation to communion, from exclusivism to inclusivism, and from insecurity to trust in God, who embraces all peoples on earth.

Bilingual Preaching and the Future of the Korean American Church

Korean preaching is clearly moving from the old to the new with the introduction of English-language services for youth in the Korean church in America. A Korean church with more than one hundred members will likely have already hired a trans-generation Korean, a Korean who was born in Korea and came to America as a child, as the youth pastor for their congregation. The trans-generation Korean is appropriate for this job, because he or she speaks both Korean and English. The trans-generation youth minister is an excellent person to lead this transition, because he or she can communicate not only with the senior Korean preacher who speaks primarily in Korean but also with the youth who speak only English. The Korean preacher who does not speak English cannot work with second-generation Koreans, who were born in America and do not speak Korean, but only English. This is why a trans-generation Korean is ideal at this stage of a church's transition. By having been born in Korea and living a part of his or her life in Korea, a trans-generation youth minister knows the Confucian propriety of respecting the old and obeying his or her superior. On the other hand, he or she also knows the Korean American youth who are acculturated to this country.

However, the gap between the Korean-speaking congregation and the English-speaking congregation within a Korean church is quite large. One significant problem that exists between the two is how they view each other. The Korean-speaking congregation treats the English-speaking congregation as if it were a mere extension of the Korean-speaking ministry. Many Korean-speaking preachers do not understand that the English-speaking youth live in a different culture with a different social outlook. In other words, Korean American youth are different from the youth who live in Korea. To treat them as an extension of the first-generation Korean congregation is a great mistake. In Korea, the youth are extensions of the adult congregation, because they speak the same language and have the same cultural orientation. However, Korean youths in America do not share the value system of first-generation Koreans and do not speak the same language.

Because English-speaking youth are treated as an extension of the Korean-speaking congregation, most Korean-speaking ministers do not grant autonomy to the younger congregants. The English-speaking ministry becomes a subsidiary to the Korean-speaking ministry. When planning programs and budgeting, the English-speaking congregation is seldom consulted. Ironically, many Korean-speaking congregations do not support the English-speaking congregation unless it adheres to the same doctrinal standards and fundamentalistic views as the Korean-speaking congregation. Moreover, most senior Korean preachers will not hire a trans-generation youth minister if he or she does not have the same doctrinal standards. Recently, I visited one of the fastest-growing Korean churches on the East Coast. The senior minister holds extremely evangelical and fundamentalistic views of the church. He hired a trans-generation youth minister who has similar views. I observed the service conducted in English. I was shocked to see the disorder in the worship service on Sunday afternoon. It was worse than a revival meeting. The youth minister, like a shaman, continuously raised the emotion of his young congregants through repetitive songs and prayers. There was no real message offered during the service, and the congregation was so emotionally charged that some spoke in tongues, and others shouted prayers. After the service, I met the senior minister and told him that the young people had become fanatic. He replied, "There is nothing wrong with being fanatic. A true Christian must be fanatic. I don't want to see my people having a lukewarm faith." Obviously, the younger congregants were acting exactly as the Korean pastor wanted and expected them to behave. Playing with young people's emotions is dangerous. This kind of practice should be strongly discouraged. In a visit to a young congregation in the Washington, D.C., area, a small group held a service that was well conducted and which included a strong message. Here was a healthy English-speaking youth group, who had been given adequate freedom to plan their own programs. The senior pastor was less authoritarian and had received his theological education from an American seminary. He allowed the youth to have an interdependent relationship with the Korean-speaking congregation.

As I have illustrated, the Korean-speaking congregation not only supports but oversees the operation of the English-speaking congregation. The relationship between the two groups is very much like the relationship between a father and son in the Confucian lifestyle. Just as the father supports the son, the Korean-speaking congregation supports the English-speaking congregation. Just as the son obeys the father, the English-speaking congregation must obey the Korean-speaking congregation. This kind of hierarchical relationship is a great hindrance for the healthy growth of an English-speaking ministry in a Korean American church.

The English-speaking congregation needs to have autonomy from the Korean-speaking congregation. However, the autonomy I speak of is not a complete separation between the two. Rather, it must be an interdependent relationship, which allows freedom and continuity. The two congregations can be both independent of and dependent upon each other. This kind of interdependent relationship is the healthiest relationship, one that both congregations will need if the Korean American church is going to succeed in the future.

What is implied when we speak of an interdependent relationship between the Korean-speaking congregation and the English-speaking congregation of a Korean church? First of all, it implies the co-equality of the Korean-speaking senior preacher and the English-speaking youth preacher. The hierarchical relationship must be replaced with an egalitarian relationship. This does not mean that the administrative hierarchy inherent in an institutional structure must be eliminated. However, in planning and in budgeting, the English-speaking preacher must have the opportunity to operate freely, just as the Korean-speaking preacher has his or her own freedom. The administrative council, consisting of both Korean-speaking and English-speaking representatives, must be allowed to approve the programs and budgets of the two groups separately, according to the needs of each congregation. This kind of structural change will help establish a healthy relationship between the two congregations. Independent budget and program for the English-speaking congregation is crucial for the success of youth ministry and for the Korean American church of tomorrow. It is important for the Korean-speaking congregation to support but not control the activities of the English-speaking congregation. There must be cominstry between the two if they are to be truly interdependent. In cominstry, each minister must be allowed his or her own distinctive doctrinal or theological orientation.

The trans-generation minister can play a key role in moving the Korean-speaking congregation into a more healthful relationship with the English-speaking congregation. However, he or she may confront enormous problems with second-generation youth, who are completely acculturated to the American way of life. The cultural gap between trans-generation and second-generation Korean Americans is as serious a gap as the one between first-generation and trans-generation Koreans in America. That is why a complete transition from a Korean-speaking congregation to an English-speaking congregation is only possible when the second generation of Korean American leadership takes charge of the English-speaking congregation. The trans-generation Korean American preacher can perform the invaluable task of introducing the cultural roots of the Korean people to the second-generation Korean Americans. Because of the importance of linking the two congregations, the trans-generation youth minister plays a pivotal role in the transition of the Korean church from the first generation to the second generation, which is the future of the Korean American church.

As the first generation makes the transition to the second generation, some of the cultural values that the first generation has held must be released. The patriarchal hierarchy which is deeply ingrained in the history of the Korean people cannot survive the test of democratic and egalitarian values which are sacred to most Americans, including second-generation Korean Americans. However, there are enduring values that second-generation Korean Americans can learn and cherish from first-generation Korean Americans. Strong family ties, respect for elders, the habit of ceaseless prayer, belief in spiritual power, a love for nature, and endurance through suffering and pain are a few of the Korean virtues that enrich the Christian faith. Although the use of the Korean language in preaching and teaching may ultimately end, many of the traditional Korean cultural activities can continue to provide distinctive aspects of social and religious programs for the second and third generations of the Korean American church. Moreover, the imaginative use of Korean culture in worship and preaching can add a distinctive flavor to the Korean American church of the future. When that creative synthesis between Korean culture and the Christian faith is integrated into the American way of life, the vision of the new Korean American church will be realized.

CHAPTER 7

KOREAN PREACHING: THE HERMENEUTIC OF LIBERATION

Although Korea has rich cultural resources from the past, Korean Christianity has rejected most of these resources as a result of its exclusive approach toward other religions. For Koreans, becoming a Protestant Christian means rejecting their former religious traditions. By rejecting traditional religions, such as shamanism, Taoism, Buddhism, and Confucianism, as heathenish, Korean Christians have been alienated from their own culture. However, no matter how much we want to cut ourselves off from our "heathenish" religious traditions, we can never be completely free of them. We are products of our past. Our attempt to be free from our past is merely an attempt to escape reality. Thus, our so-called heathenish traditions have been unconsciously integrated into our Christian life.

Some of these unconscious religious elements have greatly affected the life of the Korean church. Our spontaneous prayers on almost every occasion and our ceaseless meditation in every walk of life are deeply influenced by the Buddhist way of life. Our love of music and passionate desire for singing in the church and at other social gatherings comes from that part of our heritage rooted in indigenous religion, known as *mutang* or shamanism. Our unfailing commitment to a single book, the Bible, comes from a newer custom,

138

Christianity, brought to us by early missionaries from America. From this threefold emphasis on prayer, singing, and scripture, our ardent desire to witness Christ as our Savior has the distinctive mark of Korean preaching from the past. Aiming at the conversion of those who were heathens, Korean preaching stressed not only sin and personal repentance but also people's commitment to Christ as the only way to salvation. Because of fundamental and evangelical vigor, Korean preaching has emphasized exegetical and doctrinal sermons and neglected the contextual aspects of preaching. The shamanic ethos which was the foundation of the Korean way of life manifests itself in Korean preaching. The importance of the Holy Spirit in preaching may have been influenced by the spirituality of shamanic tradition, which stresses the charisma of a shaman.

One of the undesirable developments in Korean preaching has been its emphasis on material blessings in proportion to the faith of believers. This development may have resulted from the combination of modern materialism and shamanic inclinations. Preaching about what people want to hear and what they desire to have is one of the most grievous temptations to which Korean preachers have succumbed. Overcoming this kind of temptation in preaching is a great challenge for prophetic ministry. In spite of textually oriented sermons, most Korean preaching reflects only on the national and collective experience of suffering, oppression, and injustice. What is needed is a new hermeneutic, the hermeneutic of liberation, to reinterpret the scripture in light of the suffering and oppressive experiences of the Korean people. In order to do this, it is important for Korean preachers to liberate themselves from the fundamentalistic dogma of biblicism. This is a challenge that Korean preachers must confront in their preaching and praxis in living.

Korean preaching becomes truly distinctive when it makes use of rich cultural resources. This is possible only when we can eliminate the exclusivism which we inherited from the early missionaries, and which has been reinforced by the dualistic way of either-or thinking that is practiced in the West. When our way of thinking is transformed from the exclusive to the inclusive or open-ended way of thinking, we can truly incorporate our past religious traditions and cultural heritage into our preaching. We, as Koreans, are the embodiment of world religions, and what we are is in fact the witness of God's revelation in various religious manifestations. Thus, we are, by the very nature of our cultural endowment, pluralistic. In spite of this pluralistic nature, we can at the same time commit ourselves ultimately to Christ as our Savior. This kind of commitment within a pluralistic orientation is possible because of our open-ended approach to life, which is the very nature of the Korean heritage. For me, this ultimate commitment to Christ with an inclusive approach to pluralism is the greatest contribution that Korean preaching can make to the American church at large.

NOTES

Chapter 1: Why Korean Preaching?

1. See Soon-Myung Kim, *Korean-Americans of North America* (Seoul: Peter Books, 1991), 56.

2. Ibid.

3. In Chicago, more than 75 percent of Korean churches are categorized as small churches. Ibid., 82-83.

4. The divine presence is clearly revealed in the Word, the presence of Christ, witnessed in written words in scripture. Thus, the primary task of preaching is to interpret the biblical text in today's living situations. One of the indispensable aspects of preaching other than the congregation and the preacher is the divine presence. See Thomas G. Long, *The Witness of Preaching* (Louisville: Westminster/John Knox Press, 1989), 22-30.

5. Mearle Griffith, *A Church for the 21st Century: A Planning Resource for the Future* (Dayton, Ohio: Office of Research, the General Council on Ministries, 1989), 3.

6. See *New York Times*, April 17, 1991.

Chapter 2: Understanding the Korean Congregation Through History and Culture

1. "The bamboo tree" well illustrates the culture-specific symbolism used in preaching. See my *Sermons to the Twelve* (Nashville: Abingdon Press, 1988).

2. Jung Young Lee, "American Missionary Movement in Korea, 1882–1945: Its Contributions and American Diplomacy," *Missiology: An International Review* (American Society for Missiology) 11, no. 4 (October 1983).

3. In 1981, about 25 percent or 9,076,788 out of a total population of about 40 million Koreans were Christian. See James H. Grayson and Ruth H. Grayson, editors, *Prayer Calendar of Christian Missions in Korea and General Dictionary* (Seoul: Christian Literature Society, 1983), 219. See also

Donald N. Clark, *Christianity in Modern Korea* (Lanham, Md.: University Press of America, 1986), 1.

4. The Reverend George H. Jones, a Methodist missionary, was most instrumental in helping the unemployed Korean converts to emigrate to Hawaii. Jones went to Korea in 1887 and later was sent to Chemulpo to succeed Appenzeller in 1892. For detailed information, see Hyung-chan Kim and Wayne Patterson, eds., *The Koreans in America, 1882-1974* (Dobbs Ferry, N.Y.: Oceana Publications, 1974).

5. Won Moo Hurh and Kwang Chung Kim, "Religious Participation of Korean Immigrants in the United States," *Journal for the Scientific Study of Religion* 29 (1) (1990): 19-20.

6. Illsoo Kim, "Organizational Patterns of Korean-American Methodist Churches: Denominationalism and Personal Community," in R. E. Richey and K. E. Row, eds., *Rethinking Methodist History: A Bicentennial Historical Consultation* (Nashville: Kingswood Books, 1985), 228.

7. The official count of Korean Americans in the 1990 census was about 800,000. See Pyung Gap Min, "Korean American," in *Asian Americans: A Survey of Ethnic Groups* (New York: Department of Sociology, Queens College of C.U.N.Y., 1991), 4. But the actual number of Koreans in the United States in 1990 may have been close to one million. According to *Dong-a Daily News,* there are more than one million Koreans and over two thousand Korean churches in the United States. See "Korean Communities Are Controlled by the Korean Churches," *Dong-a Shinmoon,* October 27, 1992.

8. See Nancy Abelmann and John Lie, *Blue Dreams: Korean Americans and the Los Angeles Riots* (Cambridge: Harvard University Press, 1995), 69.

9. According to Hyung-chan Kim, the history of the Korean church in America can be divided into four main periods: The first period, 1903–1918, is marked with beginning and growth. The second period, 1919–1945, is characterized by conflicts over the policy of the church in relation to political activities. In this period, the prominent political leaders used the church as the "clubhouse" for political lectures and activities. The third period, 1945–1967, is known as the time of maintaining the status quo after the Korean liberation. This was the time when the church consisted of the new second- and third-generation Korean Americans in Hawaii. The fourth period, 1967 to the present, was marked by revival movement with the influx of immigrants through the abolition of the Oriental Exclusion Law and quota system (Acted on October 3, 1965, but the act included a three-year phase-out period). See Hyung-chan Kim, "The History and Role of the Church in the Korean American Community," Hyung-chan Kim and Wayne Patterson, eds., *The Koreans in America,* 125. However, I think that the fourth period, the revival period, continued to 1989. I suggest there is a fifth period, the period of competition and consolidation, beginning in 1990. This fifth period is also the transitional stage, where we are now as Korean Christians in America. My critical assessment on

Korean preaching is based on the fifth period with a new vision toward the twenty-first century.

10. See Illsoo Kim, "Organizational Patterns of Korean-American Methodist Churches," 234.

11. For detailed information on early missionary activities in Korea, see Jung Young Lee, "American Missionary Movement in Korea," 387-402.

12. He was a lay member of the United Presbyterian Church in Cleveland and my roommate when I was in Cleveland many years ago. Later he moved to Los Angeles. I had a chance to see him again a couple of years ago. One Sunday evening I invited him to a Korean revival service, which had been advertised in a Korean newspaper.

13. See Raymond Williams, *Religions of Immigrants from India and Pakistan: New Threads in the American Tapestry* (Cambridge: Cambridge University Press, 1988), 11; Pyong Gap Min, "The Structure and Social Function of Korean Immigrant Churches in the United States," *The International Migration Review* 26 (1992): 1382-89; Illsoo Kim, *New Urban Immigrants: The Korean Community in New York* (Princeton: Princeton University Press, 1981), 204.

14. Trans-generation Korean Americans are those who immigrated to North America involuntarily. Many children and young people came to this country because of their parents. Second-generation Korean Americans are born in America and fully acculturated to American culture. However, they are also Korean because of their biological parents and their heritage of the spiritual and cultural traditions of the Korean people. They are perfect examples of marginal persons who are neither American nor Korean, but at the same time both. See my article, "Marginality: A Multicultural Approach to Theology from an Asian-American Perspective" *Asia Journal of Theology* (October 1993): 144-53.

15. To be a Korean American means to be in between and in both worlds of Korea and America at the same time. See Jung Young Lee, *Marginality: The Key to Multicultural Theology* (Minneapolis: Fortress Press, 1995), 29-53.

16. See Jung Young Lee, "The Trend of Shamanistic Studies in America" (text in Korean), *Christian Thought* (Society for Korean Christian Literature) (December 1975), 88-93.

17. According to the Dangun myth, a female bear conceives by the heavenly being and gives birth to a son, Dangun, who fathers the Korean people. Thus the Korean people are often known as the descendants of Dangun, who connects the heavenly spirit to the earthly creatures. The continuum of spirit and matter, heaven and earth, or soul and body, is the essence of a shamanistic worldview. See Jung Young Lee, *Korean Shamanistic Rituals* (Berlin: Mouton Press, 1981), 1-26; see also Jung Young Lee, "Concerning the Origin and Formation of Korean Shamanism," in *Numen* 20, Fasc. 2 (August 1973), 135-59.

18. This story was told by my mother, who also became a Christian and denounced shamanism. Although I was fascinated by shamanic rituals at my neighbors' houses, I was often forbidden to observe them.

19. Minjung theology is closely allied with shamanism on the idea of *Han,* a grudge against injustice, which seems to be a key to understanding the relationship between minjung theology and shamanism. It is often said by minjung theologians that the shaman or *mutang* is the priest of *han.* In this area Suh Nam-dong played an important part in developing the theology of *han,* borrowing from the writings of Kim Chi-ha. See Suh Nam-dong, "In Search of Minjung Theology," trans. from Korean by Suh Kwang-sun David in his paper "Called to Witness to the Gospel Today— The Priesthood of Han," read at the consultation on the "Called to Witness" study held in Seoul, September 19-20, 1979. See also *An Emerging Theology in World Perspective: Commentary on Korean Minjung Theology,* ed. Jung Young Lee (Mystic, Conn.: Twenty-Third Publications, 1989). See also Jae Hoon Lee, *A Study of Han* (Ph.D. Dissertation at the Union Theological Seminary in New York, 1991).

20. See Dong-sik Ryu, *Hanguk Chongkyo wa Kidokkyo* (The Christian Faith Encounters the Religions of Korea) (Seoul: KCLS, 1985), 15-37.

21. Buddhism reached the northern kingdom of Koguryo A.D. 372, and by A.D. 528 it became the state religion in the Three Kingdoms. The Chinese monk known as Sundo was the first Buddhist missionary to Korea, and King Sosurim of Koguryo accepted him and built two temples for his mission. See Kim Duk-hwang, *Hanguk Chonggyo Sa* (The History of Korean Religions) (Seoul: Haemun-sa, n.d.); and Mun Sang-hi, *Hankuk Chongkyo* (Korean Religions) (Iri: Won Kwang University Press, 1973).

22. Within Neo-Confucianism, two prominent schools (Rationalism and Idealism) arose. Chu Hsi (1130-1200) was a great systematizer of the school of Rationalism, which became far more pervasive than the school of Idealism in China. In Korea, Chu Hsi's rationalism was accepted as the orthodoxy of Neo-Confucianism. For Chu Hsi's rationalism, see Fung Yu-lan, *A History of Chinese Philosophy,* vol. 2, trans. Derk Bodde (Princeton: Princeton University Press, 1953), 533-71.

23. It is often known as the "rite controversy." Most Catholic missionaries in Korea and early converts were massacred. "The first Western missionary, Father Perre Maubant, arrived in Euiju City in December 1835. Four years later he was beheaded on the sands of the Han River, along with two other European priests. In the great persecution of Christians in 1866, more than two thousand Catholics were martyred. At the end of the Catholic century (1884), about 17,500 Catholics were still alive, but they were scattered all over and had almost disappeared at the end of the period." Protestants were lucky, for when they began their work, the king of the Yi dynasty was not only weak but on the verge of its downfall. In order to rescue Korea from the encroachment of Japan, many royal families sought the assistance of American missionaries. See Jung Young Lee, "The American Missionary Movement in Korea," 388, 389-93. See also

Samuel H. Moffet, *The Christians of Korea* (New York: Friendship Press, 1962), 33-34.

24. See Jung Young Lee, "Ancestor Worship from a Theological Perspective," in Jung Young Lee, ed., *Ancestor Worship and Christianity in Korea* (Lewiston, N.Y.: Edwin Mellen Press, 1989), 90-91.

25. According to the Confucian philosophy of life, America seems to be approaching its end. It is difficult to see any American family stressing the importance of filial piety. The ideal of life in America is arranged according to horizontal relationships. The idea of democracy and equality is even applicable to the relationship between parents and children. This yields a disastrous consequence, according to Confucian teachings.

26. The symbol that represents Buddhism is known as *manja*, a reversal of the swastika. *Manja* is a cross with the ends bent at left angles.

27. For example, those who come from the southern region, known as Julla-do, have been discriminated against, just as those who came from North Korea have been. Because of this, they usually get together by themselves and form very close networks. In the life of a congregation, people from the north, from Seoul, from Taegu, and so on, often form subgroups.

28. There are three different generational groups: the first generation Koreans who immigrated to North America, the trans-generational Koreans who were brought to this country by their parents, and second- or third-generation Koreans who were born in North America. Most trans-generation Koreans speak both Korean and English, but most second-generation Koreans speak English only. English-speaking church services are provided for the second-generation and trans-generation Koreans. When the transition from Korean-speaking congregations to English-speaking congregations takes place, it creates enormous problems as well as opportunities for a unique form of ministry.

29. Many small Korean congregations in the United States can be understood as extensions of families. In many cases one or two families and their relatives make up the entire congregation. The advantage is that this creates a tight network that gives solidarity and stability. However, the disadvantage of a family-based congregation is that it is often exclusive and does not allow others to be a genuine part of congregational life.

Chapter 3: Korean Preaching in the Context of Worship Services

1. For preaching as an integral part of liturgy and a sacramental community, see Charles L. Rice, *The Embodied Word: Preaching as Art and Liturgy* (Minneapolis: Fortress Press, 1991).

2. See Charles L. Rice, *The Embodied Word: Preaching as Art and Liturgy* (Minneapolis: Fortress Press, 1991), 23; see also Fred B. Craddock, *Preaching* (Nashville: Abingdon Press, 1985), 41-44.

3. The Diamond mountains are the most beautiful mountains in Korea. There are 12,000 peaks, which resemble diamonds. They are located just

north of the 38th parallel, which divides North and South Korea. Many songs, poems, legends, and stories are written about the mountains. This visit was a rare occasion for twenty of us, who had been invited by the North Korean government to visit the mountains.

4. See Rice, *The Embodied Word,* 59-61.

5. This was the order of public service in the Korean Church of Bronx on May 10, 1992.

6. It was St. John's Korean United Methodist Church where I preached on March 3, 1994. A Korean United Methodist Church in New Jersey, which I mention here, is the Arcola Korean United Methodist Church, where I often attend. I looked at the order of public worship service when I preached on May 8, 1994. I discovered that the order was almost identical to that of other Korean churches.

7. Because most Korean churches were influenced by the Presbyterian church, the Korean Methodist church, for example, has never fully understood the Wesleyan tradition in constructing a distinctive form of liturgy.

8. See Hae-Eun Chung, "Comparison of the Liturgy Between the Korean Methodist Church and the United Methodist Church" (Unpublished MST Thesis at Drew University, 1991), 121.

9. Craddock, *Preaching,* 35.

10. According to *The Pastoral Monthly* 98 (Seoul: Walgan Ministry Press, 1984): 35, Korean churches have used the offering to build big churches, rather than for social relief work or outreach ministry. This is also true for the Korean church in the United States.

11. Craddock, *Preaching,* 44.

12. See Jung Young Lee, "Minjung Theology: A Critical Introduction," in *An Emerging Theology in World Perspective: Commentary on Korean Minjung Theology,* ed. Jung Young Lee (Mystic, Conn.: Twenty-Third Publications, 1988), 8-11.

13. Dong-sik Ryu, *The History and the Structure of Korean Shamanism* (Seoul: Yonsei University Press, 1975), 346.

14. See Jung Young Lee, *Korean Shamanistic Rituals* (The Hague, Paris, New York: Mouton Publishers, 1981), 88-91.

15. This is my translation of a song which is sung at the close of the worship service every Sunday morning at the Arcola Korean United Methodist Church in New Jersey.

16. Craddock, *Preaching,* 28.

17. Ibid.

18. Samuel H. Moffet, *The Christians of Korea* (New York: Friendship Press, 1962), 33-34.

19. Harry A. Rhodes, *History of the Korean Mission: Presbyterian Church, USA, 1884-1934* (Seoul: YMCA Press, 1934), 564.

20. See Dong-sik Ryu, *The Vein of Korean Theology* (in Korean) (Seoul: Jungmang-sa, 1982).

21. See Jung Young Lee, "Korean Christian Thought," in *The Blackwell Encyclopedia of Modern Christian Thought,* ed. Alister McGrath (Oxford: Blackwell, 1993), 309-13.

22. Paul Scott Wilson, *The Practice of Preaching* (Nashville: Abingdon Press, 1995), 210.

23. In fact, this kind of biblicism is unbiblical. As Fred Craddock says, "It is possible that a sermon that buries itself in the text, moves through it phrase by phrase, and never comes up for air may prove to be 'unbiblical' in the sense that it fails to achieve what the text achieves." See his *Preaching,* 28.

24. William Newton Blair, *God in Korea* (New York: Presbyterian Church in the U.S.A., 1957), 66-67.

Chapter 4: Distinctive Characteristics of Korean Preaching

1. Fred Craddock, *Preaching* (Nashville: Abingdon Press, 1985), 45.

2. Jung Young Lee, *Sermons to the Twelve* (Nashville: Abingdon Press, 1988), 12.

3. Fred Craddock thinks that "all preaching is to some extent self-disclosure by the preacher." See his *Preaching,* 23. Preaching as self-disclosure, Craddock says, "has a long and honorable history in the Scriptures. Accounts of being called by God were used by Jeremiah, Amos, Isaiah, and Paul to establish credentials for ministry where there was the lack of a strong supportive community. . . . Hosea and Paul [also] used their own experiences to proclaim the power and grace of God" (ibid., 208).

4. This is certainly different from the herald perspective on preaching. The preacher as the herald, is merely an instrument of the Word. He or she does not need to disclose himself or herself in preaching. The herald perspective, which was the prevalent form of homiletic in the last generation, became prominent during the neoorthodox theological movement. Karl Barth especially used the herald image in his definition of proclamation: "Proclamation is human language in and through which God Himself speaks, like a king through the mouth of his herald, which moreover is meant to be heard and apprehended." See Karl Barth, *The Doctrine of the Word of God, Church Dogmatics, I/1,* trans. G. T. Thomson (Edinburgh: T. & T. Clark, 1936), 57. Therefore, in the herald perspective, there is no genuine reciprocal relationship among the text, the preacher, the congregation, and events occurring in the world. This perspective is primarily interested in the movement *from* God *through* the herald (the preacher) *to* the hearers (the congregation). See Thomas G. Long, *The Witness of Preaching* (Louisville: Westminster/John Knox Press, 1989), 24-30.

5. Craddock, *Preaching,* 137-38.

6. This is typical exegetical preaching, which explains verse by verse. As I have noted, in exegetical sermons, "A biblical text is treated line by line, or verse by verse, to explain its meaning and relevance for today"

(Paul Scott Wilson, *The Practice of Preaching* [Nashville: Abingdon Press, 1995], 210).

7. Craddock, *Preaching*, 139.

8. Wilson, *Practice of Preaching*, 143.

9. Charles Rice, *The Embodied Word: Preaching as Art and Liturgy* (Minneapolis: Fortress Press, 1991), 75.

10. Richard L. Eslinger, *A New Hearing: Living Options in Homiletic Method* (Nashville: Abingdon Press, 1987), 123.

11. Craddock, *Preaching*, 30.

12. *Ki* in Korean is almost identical with the spirit or "ruach" in Hebrew or "pneuma" in Greek. Peter Lee, therefore, identifies *ki* or *ch'i* as the Holy Spirit. See Peter K. H. Lee, "Dancing, Ch'i, and the Holy Spirit," in *Frontiers of Asian Christian Theology: Emerging Trends*, ed. R. S. Sugirtharajah (Maryknoll, N.Y.: Orbis Books, 1994), 65-79.

13. In his well-known work, Mircea Eliade defines shamanism as the archaic techniques of ecstasy. See his *Shamanism: Archaic Techniques of Ecstasy* (New York: Bollingen Foundation, 1964).

14. Harold S. Hong, "Social, Political, and Psychological Aspects of Church Growth," in *Korean Church Growth Explosion*, ed. Bong-Rim and Marlin Nelson (Seoul: Word of Life Press, 1983), 181; Donald Clark, *Christianity in Modern Korea*, 37.

15. The importance of preaching on the suffering of Christ is quite evident in the remark of the Korean American woman who "identified with themes of Jesus' self-sacrifice, suffering and the cross as meaningful portrayals and explanations of [her life] in the U.S." See Jung Ha Kim, "Bridge-Makers and Cross-Bearers: A Case Study of Churched Korean-American Women" (Unpublished Ph.D. Dissertation at Georgia State University, 1992), 251.

16. Paul Yonggi Cho, *Mokhoe Saeng Hwal Dansang* (Reflection on Pastoral Life) 6 (Seoul, 1978), 28.

17. See Son Bong-Ho, "Some Dangers of Rapid Growth," in *Korean Church Growth Explosion*, ed. Bong-Rin Ro and Nelson Marlin (Seoul: Word of Life Press, 1983), 337-38.

18. See Jung Young Lee, "Minjung Theology: A Critical Introduction," in *An Emerging Theology in World Perspective: Commentary on Korean Minjung Theology*, ed. Jung Young Lee (Mystic, Conn.: Twenty-Third Publications, 1988), 16-18.

19. For details, see Eslinger, *A New Hearing*, 17-37, 122-25. The parable as a sermon is found in the story of "The Dandelion" in Jung Young Lee's *Sermons to the Twelve*, 15-20.

20. Jung Young Lee, *Korean Shamanistic Rituals* (The Hague, Paris, New York: Mouton Publishers, 1981), 167-69.

21. See *The Teachings of the Compassionate Buddha*, ed. with introduction and notes by E. A. Burtt (New York: New American Library, 1955), 150-54.

22. See Jung Young Lee, *Sermons to the Twelve*, 29-35.

23. Ibid., 114-15.

24. For a collection of Korean proverbs in English, see Jung Young Lee, *Sokdam: Capsules of Korean Wisdom,* 2nd ed. (Seoul: Seoul Computer Press, 1983).

25. Craddock, *Preaching,* 60.

26. Ibid., 63.

Chapter 5: The Authority of the Korean Preacher

1. See M. S. Mullinax and H. C. Lee, "Does Confucius Yet Live?: Answers from Korean American Churches" (Unpublished manuscript, Report to the annual meeting of American Academy of Religion, 1994).

2. Hee-Sung Keel, "Can Korean Protestantism Be Reconciled with Culture? Rethinking Theology and Evangelism in Korea," *Inter-Religio* 24 (Winter 1993), 47.

3. The nation in Korea is known as *Guk-ga* or the national family, which means a large family. The Christian idea of the "household of God" has a special meaning to the Korean people.

4. See Kil Jae Park, "Exploring the Openings for Ministry Based on the Congregational Study of Bethel Korean United Methodist Church" (Unpublished paper, 1993), 3.

5. Jung Ha Kim, "Bridge-Makers and Cross-Bearers: A Case Study of Churched Korean-American Women" (Doctoral Dissertation at Georgia State University, 1992), 104.

6. See Jung Young Lee, *Sermons to the Twelve* (Nashville: Abingdon Press, 1988), 87.

7. See Euntae Jo, *Korean-Americans and Church Growth* (Seoul: Cross-Cultural Ministry Institute, 1994), 114.

8. For Christ and shamanism, see Morton Smith, *Jesus the Magician* (New York: Harper, 1978); Graham H. Twelftree, *Jesus the Exorcist* (Peabody, Mass.: Hendrickson, 1995); and David Suh, "Shamanism and Minjung Liberation," in *Asian Christian Spirituality,* ed. Virginia Fabella, Peter Lee, and David Suh (Maryknoll, N.Y.: Orbis Books, 1992).

9. Donald N. Clark, *Christianity in Modern Korea* (Lanham, Md.: University Press of America, 1986), 12.

10. C. Peter Wagner, *Your Church Can Grow: Seven Vital Signs of a Healthy Church* (Ventura, Calif.: Regal Books, 1984), 65.

11. Jung Ha Kim, "Bridge-Makers and Cross-Bearers," 160.

12. Ibid., 108.

13. For an understanding of minjung theology, see Jung Young Lee, ed., *An Emerging Theology in World Perspective: Commentary on Korean Minjung Theology* (Mystic, Conn.: Twenty-Third Publications, 1988).

Chapter 6: Korean Preaching in Transition

1. "Korean Immigrants as an Isolated Island," *Kwang Ya* (Korean Harvest Mission) (July 1992), 56.

2. For preaching as a teaching event and a teaching ministry, see Clark Williamson and Ronald Allen, *The Teaching Ministry* (Louisville: Westminster/John Knox Press, 1991).

3. Preached on Thanksgiving Day, 1988, at a United Methodist church in San Diego, California.

4. See Jung Young Lee, *Sermons to the Twelve* (Nashville: Abingdon Press, 1988), 24-25.

5. See John P. Meier, *A Marginal Jew: Rethinking the Historical Jesus* (New York: Doubleday, 1991).

6. For details, see Jung Young Lee, *Marginality: The Key to Multicultural Theology* (Minneapolis: Fortress Press, 1995), 29-53.

7. The topic of the sermon, "Being a Pioneer," was based on Hebrews 11:8-16.

8. For minjung theology, see Jung Young Lee, ed., *An Emerging Theology in World Perspective: Commentary on Korean Minjung Theology* (Mystic, Conn.: Twenty-Third Publications, 1988).

9. This feeling is close to the idea of *han* in minjung theology. See Jung Young Lee, *An Emerging Theology in World Perspective*, 8-11.

10. This idea of *missio Dei* comes from Hoekendijk's theology. The essence of his thesis is: "The church lives for the world." See J. C. Hoekendijk, *The Church Inside Out*, ed. L. A. Hoekendijk and Pieter Tijmes; trans. I. C. Rottenberg (Philadelphia: Westminster Press, 1966).

11. The both-and way of thinking is explained in detail in my book, *The Theology of Change: A Christian Concept of God in an Eastern Perspective* (Maryknoll, N.Y.: Orbis Books, 1979). See also Jung Young Lee, "The Yin-Yang Way of Thinking: A Possible Method for Ecumenical Theology," *International Review of Mission* (World Council of Churches) 51, no. 239 (July 1971): 363-70.

12. See Jung Young Lee, "The Yin-Yang Way of Thinking," 363-70; Lee, *Theology of Change*; Lee, *The Trinity in Asian Perspective* (Nashville: Abingdon Press, 1996).